"Abba, Father, all things are possible unto thee."

The Gospel According to Mark, 14:35
Holy Bible

DANCING
WITH THE DEVIL

HOW PUFF BURNED THE
BAD BOYS OF HIP-HOP

MARK CURRY

NewMark Books *California*

Published by NewMark Books.
Los Angeles, California

Newmarkbooks.com

Copyright - 2009 by Mark Curry and Karl Evanzz
All rights reserved.
First Edition.

Cover Design by Do Kim
Book Design by Kanaan E. Grafix

LIBRARY OF CONGRESS CATALOGING-IN-PUBLICATION DATA

Includes bibliographic references.
ISBN: 978-0-615-27650-2

Printed in the United States of America

10 9 8 7 6 5 4 3 2 1

Ex Libris

DEDICATION

In loving memory to my mother, Lillie Curry, and my father, Elma Kenneth Curry, who taught me the importance of believing in God, in them, in family, and in myself. It's also dedicated to Dee Dee, my son Mark Jr., and to my siblings.

CONTENTS

CHAPTER 1

Fame

It's a funny thing, fame. One day you're on top of the world, sipping Cristal while composing a song aboard a private jet bound for Jamaica. A year or two later, you're drinking Mad Dog 20/20 and flipping burgers in Hell's Kitchen.

As an artist on the Bad Boy Entertainment label, I spent the last decade traveling around the world to entertain fans of hip-hop music. I've been in million-dollar music videos. I've recorded with some of the biggest names in music, including David Bowie, Jimmy Page, Snoop Dogg, and Busta Rhymes. I've attended more celebrity events than I can remember. There were parties that I'd like to recall but can't because my memory was compromised by too much alcohol and drugs. Fame can be a sneak-peek into heaven or a premonition of hell, and on occasion can feel like both at the same time.

"Oh my God, I know you! I saw you in a video!" two teenagers ran up to me and said when they saw me shopping with my son at a local mall. I smiled and thanked them for acknowledging me and tried to leave it at that. But the questions shifted to topics that take too long to explain while snacking at the food court or standing in the checkout line at Foot Locker.

"How did you become a Bad Boy?" they asked. "How did you meet Diddy? What's Kim Porter like?"

They wanted to know about the "real" Sean John Combs, the man formerly known a Puffy, then Puff Daddy, then P-Diddy, and then Diddy. David Letterman once joked that Puff changes his name so often that it's only a matter of time before he'll be known as "Yankee Doodle Diddy." To keep things simple, I'll call him Puff, his current preference.

I first met Puff in early 1995 when he was "Puff Daddy," a Harlem record producer who was largely unknown outside of music circles. That April, one of the hottest new nightclubs in Atlanta opened on West Peachtree in Midtown. Although owned on paper by Barbara Cooke, Platinum House was run by two of my buddies, Chris and Vee. Barbara was the widow of Sam Cooke. Vee married Barbara's granddaughter, Nicole Alexander, in 1994.

Designed to attract a national celebrity clientele, Platinum House was a success out of the starting gate. First, Vee hired some of the finest exotic dancers in Atlanta. Then he hired an interior designer who created a set which rivaled the best from Hollywood. The building itself resembled a castle. Platinum House was a black version of Studio 54 without the kinkiness, and with dancers paid to shed their clothing. The combination guaranteed that men would leave home even in cold weather to lust and spend a shipload of cash.

To hype the club, Vee made an arrangement with Bad Boy Entertainment to host "Bad Boy Fridays" at Platinum. The parties were managed by Anthony "Wolf" Jones, a longtime friend and personal bodyguard for Puff. Jones was known as "Wolf" partly because his hairstyle reminded people of Eddie "Wolfgang" Munster, Herman's little hell-raiser. The other reason is that people said his attitude reminded them of "the big bad wolf" in fairy tales. He was known for his quick temper and his crafty, wise-guy ways.

Puff and his entourage attended many of the Bad Boy Fridays; sometimes the whole Bad Boy roster showed up. I didn't pay Puff too much attention at the time because he wasn't really a celebrity in those days.

Vee hired me to work the door as an identification checker. It wasn't the job I had in mind when he first offered me employment, but it was still a great opportunity because it put me in a position to meet the biggest names in Black music. Everybody tried to get in. You'd be amazed at what people will do to gain access to celebrities, and I've seen it all.

We hosted a couple of parties for Bobby Brown, the former lead singer of New Edition. After a few weeks, I noticed that Bobby often arrived with a dude named Eddie whom I knew from way back. Eddie lived in College Park then, and was a well-known drug dealer. He sold death by the capsule, by the bag, by the puff, and any other way you wanna take drugs. So the minute I saw Eddie with Bobby and noticed how out of it Bobby looked, I understood better why he had become an "old edition."

The tabloids were having a field day with his erratic public behavior and all the "baby mama" drama that was jeopardizing his marriage to Whitney Houston. There were rumors that Whitney was going to leave him. She had already stopped paying the mortgage on his mansion, the one formerly owned by Michael Thevis, the so-called "Scarface of Porn." (Thevis controlled most of the pornography business throughout the country from that mansion). Despite his money problems, Bobby had so many hangers-on that even his leeches had leeches.

In the early fall, Platinum House hosted an after party during a big birthday bash weekend for Atlanta-based record mogul Jermaine

Dupri. Celebrities came from all across the country. Marion "Suge" Knight of Death Row Records blew into town with his posse, including his longtime friend and bodyguard, Jai Hassan-Jamal Robles, known in the streets as "Big Jake." Suge and Jake had been friends for ages, and the fact that Jake had just gotten out of prison two days earlier gave the celebration a double meaning for them.

Puff was there as usual with his crew, among them Jason Brown and Wolf, his childhood friends. Wolf was Puff's full-time bodyguard.

This night at the Platinum attracted members of the two largest gangs in Los Angeles, the Crips and the Bloods, who had been moving into Atlanta since the late 1980s. Some of them had money as a result of large-scale drug dealing. Some were Bloods who were in the money through their ties to Suge, no stranger to Atlanta because he was once a bodyguard for Bobby Brown. Others were Crips who afforded the high life through their secret connections to Bad Boy's echelon. To make matters worse, tensions were building between Puff and Suge.

A month before the party, Suge insulted Puff in front of thousands of celebrities inside Madison Square Garden's Paramount Theater at *The Source* magazine's second annual Hip Hop Music Awards. Puff has an annoying habit of inserting himself into the songs and videos of all the artists on his label, and it was common knowledge that many Bad Boy acts resented him for this. Asked about the practice in the July 1995 issue of a magazine aimed at black teenagers, Puff said: "I like performing with my artist, I like talking on the records, and I like being in videos."

But he also revealed an ulterior motive. "It protects my interests in terms of what I'm going to do in the future. Say if a company tries to remove me. It's going to be hard to remove me and still have all my acts and the same level of intensity and the same flavor and feeling."

Even worse, Puff charged the artists for his appearances on their records and videos, usually without them realizing it until they received their paltry publishing royalty statements. That's when they discovered that a large sum of their money had gone to fees which were doubled, tripled and even quadrupled because of Puff's "special guest appearance." He charged artists, for example, for having his

Bentley in their videos – which he insisted upon – then took a tax credit for business use of the car.

A few had complained publicly that Puff was upstaging them as much as he was promoting them. They felt that his presence was more of a distraction than an attraction since critics considered Puff a mediocre rapper and marginal dancer at best. They pointed out that you never saw Suge making himself the focus of videos by artists on Death Row, and you never saw Russell Simmons fronting on Def Jam videos. On the other hand, you never saw a Bad Boy video or heard a Bad Boy rapper without a cameo by Puff.

While accepting a special award, Suge castigated Puff for being such a publicity pimp. Staring in Puff's direction, Suge said:

"To all you artists out there who don't wanna go on a record label where the executive producer's all up in the videos, all on the records, dancing, then come to Death Row!" Since Suge was on Puff's turf in New York, East Coast rappers felt disrespected. No sooner had Suge finished his statement than Puff's supporters retorted with "Fuck the West Coast!"' and "East Coast, East Coast!"

Young men dressed like gang-bangers rose from their seats and got ready to rumble, but emcee Ed Lover rushed to the mike and tried to embarrass everybody into behaving. "When you watch the Grammies and American Music Awards, you complain about how they [mis]represent hip-hop," Lover said like a daddy disappointed with his kids. "Don't fuck this award show up!"' Snoop Dogg, Dr. Dre, and Puff also rushed to the podium and asked the audience to chill, which they did.

Despite the appearance of unity and calm, Suge's comments stung Puff, but they also triggered a geographical dividing line between rappers on the two coasts. In failing to respond to Suge's aspersions, Puff lost the respect of a lot of young hip hop fans that night. He had been called a chump by his equal and failed to refute it.

Into this already explosive mix were some ill-informed brothers who had female issues. I'm talking about dudes who have a "that's my bitch" mentality, those who regard every woman not related to them as a slave or an animated sex toy.

Anyway, as Bad Boys gathered in one corner at Platinum House, Nicole and Wolf chatted by the downstairs bar. Nicole was raised among black music's royalty, so she's not the type of woman who'll tolerate being disrespected. In addition to being Sam Cooke's granddaughter, she is the stepdaughter of famed Motown singer Mary Wells. When Mary Wells was down and out and living in South Central, one of the neighborhoods she lived in was controlled by Bloods, and one of the Bloods that Nicole knew personally was none other than Suge.

Wolf kept his cool as Suge and Jake approached Nicole. Suge stood to Nicole's right, while Jake stood on Wolf's left. Wolf refused to acknowledge either of them.

"So, you out here doin' these East Coast niggas now, huh," Suge said. "You're doin' all these Bad Boy parties?"

Nicole looked at them contemptuously and kept talking to Wolf, who was facing her. She knew that Vee loved her and wasn't about to let someone come into their club and disrespect either them or their customers. Vee pretended not to be watching but he was on Suge like wet on water.

Jake became infuriated that neither Wolf nor Nicole seemed fearful of him, so he started going ape-shit. "This is Bompton Piru! This is Bompton Piru up in this muthafucka!" (Bloods refer to Compton as "Bompton" because they claim to own it, and Piru is the name of one of the streets in their territory.) Suge and Jake weren't aware of it, but they might as well have been standing in front of the O.K. Corral in Tombstone. You could sense the Grim Reaper's presence. I don't remember now if the music actually stopped, but it seemed like the only thing that I could hear was Jake yelling and screaming about getting respect.

Jake was so focused on Wolf that he didn't realize that Jason had no intention of letting them harm Wolf. He and Wolf had been close since their teenage years, when they were part of a group that Puff rolled with called the Valley Mob. He hadn't said a word the whole time, but you could see that he was sizing up the situation, figuring out if Suge had other supporters there to back him up. Vee sensed what was happening, too. He stepped in between them and said: "That ain't goin' down here in this Club."

To restore calm, he ordered Suge and Big Jake to leave. Vee told Chris Howard, a Fulton County Sheriff's deputy who was moonlighting as a security guard, to escort them out of the club and to their limousine. Suge looked at Vee like he was ready to kick his ass or something, but his threatening stare rolled off Vee like sweat off a slave. A bully always takes a gamble with his life when he decides to intimidate someone, and Vee would have been a deadly bet.

"Why y'all disrespectin' my house like this, Suge? We don't come out to the MOB (Suge's nightclub in Las Vegas) doing this to y'all. You calling me a Crip and my wife a traitor."

In my book, the first person to leave the premises in the heat of an argument is the person you have to watch out for, and Jason sneaked out while Suge was talking to Vee.

As Suge and Jake walked out of the club to get into a limo that was parked out front, Puff arrived by limousine. Wolf was on his cell phone trying to call Puff to warn him that there was trouble at the club and that he should stay away.

"We're not going in there!" Wolf yelled over the growing noise and sporadic fighting among the factions. "Fuck it. We're outta here."

But before Wolf could make his way to the limousine to talk to Puff, Jason whipped out his pistol and pumped a piece of lead into Jake's 300-pound frame. The bullet hit him in the stomach. Jake pressed his left arm against his stomach, turned around and dived into the limo, but Jason got off two more rounds before the car door closed. Both shots struck Jake in his buttocks. While Jason was shooting, he was staring at Suge like he was saying: "Nigga, you know this should have been you."

Puff emerged from the limo and approached Suge. "Is everything all right, man? Are you okay?"

As Puff moved closer to Suge, who had nothing to lose but his life, Suge quickly grabbed Puff in a choke hold and used him for a shield as he backed into the doorway of the club. Although Puff and Suge are both almost six feet tall, Suge outweighs him by at least a hundred pounds, the result of beefing up for professional football a long time ago. Puff kept saying, "I don't have nothing to do with that Suge, I don't have nothing to do with that". Once inside, Suge let Puff go.

"Oh my God . . . muthafuckas," Suge kept repeating.

Vee was outside trying to save Jake's life by applying pressure to his stomach area where blood was gushing out. He kept talking to him, assuring him that everything would be all right. Suge was running around in circles ranting and raving like a rooster, but wasn't doing shit to actually help save Jake's life.

"Breathe, Brother, breathe," Vee said.

"Am I hit bad?" Jake asked him like a frightened kid talking to his father. The look of doom was on his face.

"Naw, man," Vee replied, "you're straight . . . just try to relax and breathe."

Big John, another security guard, squeezed Vee's left shoulder. Vee looked around but maintained the pressure on Jake's abdomen.

"What?" Vee asked.

"Come on, man, let him go. This ain't your problem." Vee ignored Big John. They didn't seem to get it. Vee didn't want anyone dying in his new club, especially if he could do something to prevent it. Besides, he told me later, he'd want someone to do the same for him if he was trapped in enemy territory and his life was hanging in the balance.

Puff stood on the sidewalk with a couple of his guards. Once the crowd dispersed, Suge came out of the club and started yelling at Puff. "This ain't over, nigga, this ain't over. You know what this is about."

"You need to tend to your man, Dog." Puff replied. "Tend to your man."

Everyone started to disperse as several police cruisers arrived. As the ambulance took Jake away, police questioned the people who didn't get away fast enough, but of course everybody said that they hadn't seen anything.

Jake made it to the hospital alive, but he was in critical condition.

CHAPTER 2

One In a Million

The whole city was buzzing about the shooting after it made the nightly news. Jason and Wolf kept low profiles while police continued interviewing witnesses, several of whom mistakenly identified Wolf as the shooter. Adding fuel to the fire, someone started a rumor that Wolf was Puff's cousin. In the meantime, Puff returned to New York and Suge retreated to Los Angeles.

Suge had a reputation for getting on a soapbox and preaching about the unbreakable bond between Bloods, but his actions suggested that it was nothing more than talk. On one occasion when Vee was at

Grady Memorial Hospital visiting Jake, a nurse asked him why no one else seemed concerned – no visits, no "get well" cards or flowers, no phone calls, no nothing.

Vee was surprised. Then he noticed that the only flowers in Jake's room were the ones that he and Nicole brought. With so many Bloods rumored to be living in Atlanta, you would think that Suge would have ordered or paid someone to visit Jake daily, or to at least check on him every once in a while. No one did.

As Jake's life hung in the balance in Atlanta, a young black man from Los Angeles claiming to represent Death Row contacted Mark Bell, one of Puff's longtime friends who handled promotional work for Bad Boy Entertainment. The caller said that Bell would get a lucrative contract promoting Death Row artists if he played his cards right.

"What do you mean?" Bell asked.

The caller told Bell to jot down the home address for Puff, and for Janice Combs, Puff's mother, on a piece of paper and fold it. Then, the caller said, Bell should go outside of the office building where he worked and pretend to take a cigarette break or something. After a few minutes, he said, Bell should drop the folded piece of paper on the ground and then return to his office.

Bell had known Janice Combs since he was in junior high school. She was like an aunt, so he wasn't about to entertain the offer. But rather than reject the proposition outright and possibly face the well-known wrath of Suge Knight, Bell told the caller that he had no idea where either Puff or Janice Combs lived. He hung up, hoping that would be the end of the matter.

A week or so after Jake was hospitalized, Vee came to Platinum House looking like a damn zombie. I thought he was sick, so I asked him if he felt okay.

"Naw, man," he said while staring into his drink. "I just came back from the hospital. That brother ain't gonna make it."

"For real?" I asked somewhat in disbelief. My mind drifted back to the night of the shooting as Vee began to answer.

"Yeah. You can see it in his eyes. It's like he's already dead. This sister who's a nurse over there told me that they're just waiting for orders to turn the machines off."

"Damn, man. I'm sorry to hear that."

Vee had done everything he could to save Jake's life that night. Although he had never met Jake before and even considered him a possible enemy that fateful night, he felt sorry for him. A turn of events and Jake could have been him or anyone else in the club, Vee said. Jake, like a million other young men trapped in America's ghettos, could have turned his life around once he got out of prison. Instead, he put his life on the line to protect a friend whom he worshiped. Now, as he faced his darkest hour, Suge was nowhere to be found.

Jake's plight made me think about something that one of my favorite pastors used to say to warn us about gang violence.

"There's an old saying," the preacher said. "When you smile, the whole world smiles with you; but when you cry, you cry alone."

I imagined Jake being in that room hooked up to all those beeping machines, hoping to hear a familiar voice or to see a family member's face one last time. Vee confided in me that he would talk to Jake just to let him know that not everyone in the world had forgotten him.

Vee had such a mean reputation in the streets that I was surprised to see this side of him. A friend who works for an ambulance service said that Vee was having a natural reaction to saving someone's life. When you give CPR to someone who would have died otherwise, your emotions get involved and you want to see that person survive. If they survive, you feel like a hero. But if they don't, sometimes you feel like you failed them.

Platinum House was also struggling to survive. Trouble was coming from every direction. The cops were hounding patrons, the media kept rehashing the story, there were rumors about retaliation from Suge, and everybody who came into the club kept asking the same questions: "Have you heard anything from Suge? Did that dude die?"

As business slowed to a trickle, Vee and Chris closed Platinum for a week and were talking about shutting down for good. I needed the income, but I understood where they were coming from. People get superstitious when somebody dies at a club.

Fortunately, I had another job to fall back on. I told them to call me when they were ready to open up again. During the day, I washed cars at The Rim Shop, one of the most popular car accessories boutiques in Atlanta. Located on northeast Peachtree, the shop's clientele included the biggest names in hip hop. But it also attracted underworld types.

One of them was this crazy Cuban cat named Butta who regularly came into the shop to get top-of-the-line car toys. This guy was new to the States, and rumor had it that he was part of a powerful cocaine cartel.

In February 1993 Butta came into the shop and asked one of my co-workers if he wanted to join him and some of his friends for the NBA's all-star Game in Salt Lake City. At first Travis thought he was kidding, but when he showed us the tickets to the game and to the plane, we knew this dude was a major player. I kid you not, I didn't see Travis again for almost three years. When I did, he was still talking about how Jordan, Malone, Barkley, Stockton, and Shaq turned the place out in an overtime nail-biter.

Travis had done well by Butta, but Butta's luck finally ran out and he got deported. Travis returned to Atlanta to collect money owed to Butta by people in the game. He was wealthier but not much wiser, even though he considered himself a bona fide "wise guy" now. He was collecting serious money, too, but the minute he got it, he had to hand it off to somebody else.

One night he showed up at Platinum House talking so fast and crazy that I thought he was having a nervous breakdown. A drug connection whom he had met through Butta had vanished. To keep the drugs flowing, the cartel wanted him to do the work that the missing guy was supposed to handle. To ensure his cooperation, the cartel kidnapped his sister, who was also the mother of a popular teenage hip hop artist. They threatened to kill her if Travis didn't cooperate. He pleaded for my help, and offered to pay me $12,000 in cash if I could get his sister back.

The first person that came to mind was a gang banger from Los Angeles who now lived in Atlanta, a guy named Jay-D. I met Jay-D through Vee. Jay-D had a relative whom everybody called Cuz. One day Cuz, who was tight with Vee, called Vee and asked him to let Jay-D hide out in Atlanta for a spell because Jay-D had such an itchy trigger finger that people were shooting at him in the streets and trying to do drive-bys on his crazy ass. Vee agreed.

Anyway, we left the club and picked up Jay-D. After Travis described two cars with Florida license plates – a white Buick and a blue Mercedes – we took him home and told him to lay low. Jay-D and I drove all over the city looking for the Colombians. After four or five hours with no luck, I called Travis and gave him the bad news.

"Why don't you call your connection and tell him that you want to meet him somewhere to talk things over?" I suggested. "Tell him that you're willing to work for them if certain conditions are met." After we figured out what those conditions would be, Travis called the contact's beeper.

Once the Colombian called him back from a pay phone with the rendezvous point, Jay-D and I headed straight there. The rendezvous point was a hotel on Riverdale Road in Forest Park. Sure enough, the two cars arrived about five minutes after we did.

I called Travis back and told him to beep the Colombians again and say that he was having major transportation problems and that it would take him another hour to get a different car. They agreed. They parked the Mercedes in the parking lot of a busy shopping center and left in the Buick. Keeping our distance, we tailed them back to their hotel in nearby Jonesboro. We were sure that Travis' sister was inside.

"Watch out for me," Jay-D said as he hopped out of the car and grabbed a 12-gauge shotgun from a hidden compartment in the back seat.

"Goddamn, Homes, are you crazy!" I yelled as my heart pounded against my chest. This fool was about to get both of us killed, either by the cops or by the vicious-ass Colombians. "We ain't got no battle plan. We don't know who else is in there with her or what they're carrying. We need to plan this shit right."

Jay-D reluctantly agreed.

"Let's go pick up my partner who lives over on Bankhead," I suggested. "This is right up his alley. He loves this kind of shit." Picking up Li'l Rick would mean that I'd have to split that $12,000 three ways instead of two, but at least I'd still be alive, I thought as Jay-D headed over to the West Side of town.

Li'l Rick had his own crew. He borrowed a tow truck from a friend, and then put a car on its bed. Inside the car were five of his friends armed to their teeth. The reward started to look less and less attractive now that our number had quadrupled.

In our rush to organize, we naturally assumed that the Colombians would still be at the hotel when we returned. But the hour was nearly gone by the time we left the West Side, so I called Travis once again and told him to beep his connection. Every time he beeped them, they would call back from a different pay phone near their hotel.

We parked the two trucks outside the hotel in Jonesboro and waited. After five minutes or so, the same two men whom we saw getting into the Buick earlier emerged from their room and walked toward their car in the parking lot. I sat back as the lookout man; all I had to do was blow the horn if I saw anything that threatened the plan.

Once they were within a few feet of the Buick, Jay-D jumped out and pointed the shotgun at the Colombians. "Get down! Get on the ground muthafuckas!" he barked as the two men obeyed.

The five dudes hiding in the car on the tow truck revealed themselves and trained their weapons on the kidnappers. While they held them at gunpoint, Li'l Rick and Jay-D went into the room and got Travis' sister. They also took a shoe box filled with money and some drugs from a plastic bag inside a suitcase.

They ran back outside and Jay-D jumped into the car. He tossed a shoe box on the floor next to me and held the shotgun on the Columbians as we sped away. Li'l Rick drove away in the opposite direction.

Sister was fairly composed for someone who had just been rescued from almost certain death. She was unharmed through the whole ordeal. We met Travis at a gas station on Dr. Martin Luther King Jr. Drive. He was in tears as he embraced his sister.

"You know y'all gonna have to leave town for a while," I said.

"Shoot, man," Travis replied, "you ain't gotta worry about that. We're getting the hell out of here tonight."

Although we knew that the Columbians would be looking for us, we were so happy about having so much money that we went to a strip club and blew a wad of big bills. We bought cell phones and rented five hotel suites for the night.

The next morning, my pager went off around seven o'clock. It was an urgent message from Chris.

He said that Vee had been very depressed since the death of Big Jake on October 6, so he wanted to get him out of town for a while. They had decided to attend the Million Man March in Washington. With Jakes's death and the downturn at Platinum House, Chris said that maybe the march would be reinvigorating.

I don't know if Chris's call was coincidence or fate. Whatever it was, the timing was impeccable. Vee needed to refocus and I needed to get out of Atlanta because of the Colombians. The march gave me a million and one reasons. I told him that I'd be ready to go anytime, and asked whether Jay-D could tag along. Chris said that would be no problem as long as we could leave town before sundown.

He rented a dark-blue Cadillac Deville. I called Jay-D, who said he had been praying for a way to attend the march. Chris pulled up at ten o'clock, and the four of us were on the highway a few minutes later.

The shoe box that Jay-D took from the Colombians contained almost $55,000. After paying for the hotel rooms, expenses at the strip club, and giving Li'l Rick $10,000 to split with his crew, Jay-D and I had about $40,000. We split the money and bought two small black bags to keep each of our shares in, and told Travis to keep the reward money. Though Jay-D's bag was much fuller than mine, it didn't matter to me because it was all free money.

It seems like everybody from Atlanta who visited Washington came back talking about all the high class stores in Tyson's Corner, Virginia, so that was our first stop as we neared the nation's capital. Sure enough, there were stores there with every name in fashion that you could think of. Gianni Versace was hot in 1995 and Jay-D was crazy about his stuff. He went into the Versace boutique and bought a dozen shirts but only one suit.

On October 16, 1995, African-American men from across the nation gathered on the National Mall for the Million Man March to support "unity, atonement and brotherhood." When we arrived at the mall, most of the black men were in casual clothing. Jay-D looked like he was headed to an exclusive party in Palm Beach.

There was some dispute about the number of people there, but it sure felt like a million. Minister Louis Farrakhan, the Nation of Islam's leader who spearheaded the march, was well-respected among black men. But his decision to confine the march to men of color had angered many black women. Some black men did not particularly like the messenger, but it was impossible to argue with his message. "It's time for us to clean up our lives and rebuild our communities," he said.

I had never seen so many black people before in my life. For the first time, I had a sense of what it must have been like to participate in all the huge protest marches of the 1960s or to attend the 1964 March on Washington. As I looked around, I completely forgot about what had transpired in Atlanta a few nights earlier, and even forgot about the money waiting for me back at the hotel. I felt like I was in heaven – a Black Heaven – but heaven just the same. There were members of rival gangs standing shoulder to shoulder, yet no one threw a punch. I witnessed brothers, uncles, and neighbors who hadn't spoken to each other in ages finally mend their differences that day, and I beamed with pride when I saw Asians, Native Americans, and Latino brothers among us.

Most of us stood in place for hours, but no one complained. A I looked around me, I couldn't help but wondering for a hot minute about what would happen if a couple of hothead gang bangers started something. Even though the fight would have involved only a handful of people, the entire crowd of one million would have been blamed. There were no tanks in sight, but I knew that a lot of us would have died right there on the Mall. I'm sure that military helicopters would have begun dropping something lethal on us lickety-split.

The crowning moment for me came after we recognized several Muslims that we knew standing onstage near Minister Farrakhan.

Farrakhan's son, Mustafa, was a regular customer at the Rim Shop, as were members of his security team, who primarily drove armored Lincoln Town cars. Once we contacted the security team leader by phone, he sent an escort who took us all the way through the crowd and behind the stage.

As we climbed the stairs to the stage, I felt like a king or foreign dignitary, forgetting the fact that I was just an average Joe. From there, he found a section for us on stage to Farrakhan's right. We were so close to Farrakhan that I could actually see a reflection in the bulletproof glass. As thousands of cameras clicked away, I felt like I was in a dream.

But I also I found myself wondering about how vulnerable Farrakhan and the other black leaders were in spite of all that security. The friend who took us to the stage trusted us, and he had no reason not to. But when it comes to protecting someone so important to his people or to his country, a guard in that position has to be as vigilant as the Secret Service.

CHAPTER 3

Karma

Chris and Vee decided to spend a few more days in Washington, so they asked me and Jay-D to return the rented Cadillac to Atlanta. Jay-D volunteered to take responsibility for the car and promised Vee that he would return it promptly. Shortly after noon we loaded up the Cadillac, including the money remaining after a night of partying and drinking Moet so expensive that the waiter had to wipe dust off the bottles.

After driving the first stretch of the trip, I handed the wheel over to Jay-D and took a nap. When I woke up about four hours later, I discovered that he had missed a crucial turn off Highway 85 and that we were now three hours off course and by the beach in South Carolina. I lost it and yelled at him for a second, then told him that I would drive the rest of the way.

When we finally reached my house, I reminded Jay-D to return the car promptly as he had promised. The next day, he came into the shop with a worried look on his face, and I knew immediately that he had broken his word and had done something stupid.

"I totaled the car, man," he said. "I was taking the car back and was damn near there when this asshole ran right smack into me."

The only ones insured to drive the car were Chris and Vee.

"Damn, Jay-D, Vee is gonna shit in his pants when he hears that," I said. "That car was brand new, man."

I was trying to figure out what to do when I remembered the money that we had taken from the Colombians. I always had a bad feeling about the money because it had come too easily. In the back of my mind I kept expecting something bad might to happen because we had been blessed in rescuing Sister without anyone getting hurt, but we took advantage of the blessing by ripping those dudes off. They say that two wrongs don't make a right, so I felt like we might have displeased God. I didn't say anything, though, because I didn't want them thinking that I was a wimp or something.

"How much money do you have left?" I asked.

"Uh . . . maybe about $5,000," Jay-D replied.

"Man, don't bullshit me," I shot back. "You had damn near $15,000 yesterday. You gonna have to give Vee some money for the car or you're gonna wish you had. Vee plays for keeps and he ain't no damn fool. You fucked up and you know it. If I didn't owe you one, I'd walk away and let all the weight fall on you, man, because you should have turned that car in like you promised. I'll chip in $5,000, but you have to give me whatever you have left – at least $10,000. We'll put it aside until Vee gets back."

I called Vee and told him about the car. He went through the roof, as I expected, so I tried to calm him down by offering him the money. He told me to hold onto the money but not to turn in the car yet since there was no police report about the accident. I don't how he did it, but Vee settled with the rental car company and gave me half of my money back after I promised him that I wouldn't tell Jay-D.

Big Jake's body was shipped to Los Angeles for burial a few days before I returned to Atlanta. By the time Vee and Chris returned to Atlanta on October 20, rumors were flying about Suge's plans to avenge Jake's death. Even before the march, Suge had been telling people that Puff was a devil who arranged the shooting to strike at Suge for calling him a chump at *The Source* magazine awards show. And even though the cops hadn't arrested anyone for Jake's death, they were still looking for Wolf. Word on the street was that when Suge heard about the close bond between Jason and Puff, he went ballistic.

With police cruising around the Platinum House nearly every night, it became difficult to attract national celebrities, or much of anyone for that matter. Worse, Jason dropped by periodically in the wee hours of the morning to buy a couple of bottles of Cristal. It would be 3 o'clock and all of a sudden Vee would hear someone banging on the door. If he didn't open it, Jason would just keep banging on it. Fearing that the noise would attract police, Vee would simply open the door after he realized that Jason would never go away without that Cristal.

Jason already had a reputation for being lethal before Jake's death, so nobody was about to finger him as the actual trigger man. While Wolf remained in hiding, a landmark rite of passage forced Jason above ground.

On a Saturday night about five months after Jake died, Jason was at the Magic City strip club on Forsyth Street with friends who were throwing him a bachelor's party. There were a couple of different versions of what happened, but no one disputes that a cop moonlighting as a security guard shot him three times in the back. Rumor had it that Suge had arranged Jason's murder, but another story emerged after Jason's fiancé filed a wrongful death action.

In the $10 million lawsuit filed after Jason's death was ruled a justifiable homicide, Sharonda Davis said that she and Jason had planned to get married later that day. Jason was leaving the party when two dudes in a car exiting the parking lot started trouble. Jason and the men got into an argument which led to a gunfight. Jason spotted the security guard and ran, but the guard shot him. According to Davis, the cop tear-gassed Jason while he was down. The biggest problem with Sharonda's version was that she wasn't there, so all of her information was second-hand, and the cop's lawyers tore her account apart.

The cop said that due to a bottleneck at the exit from the club, drivers in either lane had to alternate leaving the parking lot. When it was Jason's turn to exit, the driver in the adjacent lane refused to let him go and instead sped up and exited first. This angered Jason and a shouting match ensued. After Jason exited the parking lot, he followed the car. When he spotted it, he ran over to the car and pointed his gun at the two men and apparently was about to shoot when he spotted the cop.

Once he saw the cop pointing the gun at him, he aimed his gun at the cop in an attempt to make the cop run for cover. However, the cop stood his ground, so Jason turned around and ran. That's when the cop gave chase and killed him. After hearing the cop's version, the court threw out the fiancé's lawsuit because Georgia law allows a cop to use deadly force once a suspect aims a gun at him.

Anyone who thought that things would cool off after Jason's death was mistaken. Despite rumors of Suge's involvement, there was no proof. Indeed, Suge must have felt cheated by Jason's death because it denied him a chance to kill Jake's killer and of the opportunity to exact revenge from Puff, whom he believed put Jason up to it.

Despite Jason's death, Suge was still determined to strike back. He got lucky two months after Jake died. Mark Bell had forgotten about the mysterious telephone call from Los Angeles by the time Roderick Nixon, a trusted friend, mentioned that he was attending Death Row's annual Christmas party in Hollywood Hills. An hour or so after midnight, Suge entered the Chateau Le Blanc mansion with a posse of bodyguards and friends, among them Tupac Shakur and Dr. Dre.

As Suge made his way through the large crowd, he spotted Bell. Bell nervously walked over to him and mumbled something about it being a great party and said how much he was interested in the earlier offer to work for Death Row.

"Why didn't you cooperate with me when you had the chance, nigga?"

Bell assured him that he didn't know where either Puff or Janice Combs lived. As Suge raised his voice and gave Bell a threatening stare, Suge's entourage surrounded them. "Follow me," Suge commanded as Bell was forced upstairs.

After entering an office in the mansion, Suge placed two chairs in the middle of the room. He sat in one as a NFL-size bodyguard pushed Bell onto the other one. Dr. Dre, Tupac and the rest of the entourage formed a ring around the chairs. Another burly bodyguard wearing a cheesy gold grill over his teeth punched Bell in the face and said, "This is for Jake." Bell didn't know what the hell he was even talking about.

As Suge left the room carrying an empty wine flute, the bodyguard continued to rough up Bell. "We're going to kill you," he threatened. "You're gonna pay for what happened to Jake."

Suge returned a few minutes later. The wine flute was full now with a yellowish liquid that had a few small bubbles on top. As Suge ordered him to drink it, Bell immediately noticed that it was urine and turned his face in the opposite direction.

"Drink it if you wanna live, bitch," Suge demanded. The bodyguard punched the captive in his face again.

Bell accepted the flute from Suge as though he planned to drink it. As the circle of onlookers relaxed and even began to laugh at what they believed was about to transpire, Bell threw the flute on the floor and rushed through the open French doors leading to the balcony. He was halfway over the guardrail before Suge and the gang caught up with him. They grabbed and punched him as he was dragged back to the center of the room.

After several men fell on top of him, Bell could see Tupac among those kicking him. Goldie (the bodyguard with the grill) choked Bell until he finally recognized that if he didn't play dead, he was gonna be dead. He pretended to be unconscious by lying still, but his ruse was undone once Goldie kicked him in his testicles. Suddenly, a member of the entourage walked over to Suge and whispered something in his ear.

Suge ordered a halt to the beating and helped Bell to his feet. For some odd reason, he began giving Bell the "good cop" routine.

"Things don't have to be this way," the record mogul said. "I can make you rich. Don't you wanna make a half-million dollars?" Suge escorted Bell to the bathroom as he continued to offer him various options for getting rich.

After Bell cleaned himself up and entered the hall just outside the bathroom, Suge's sudden change of heart became apparent. Several bodyguards were listening to police radio transmissions. Bell overheard someone say that police were entering the mansion. As it turned out, Nixon was watching as Bell was taken upstairs. He watched to see which room they took Bell into. And fortunately for Bell, he was outside and saw Bell trying to escape his captors. When Nixon saw the incident on the balcony, he dialed 911.

LAPD officers entered the mansion just as Bell was being taken back downstairs. A female officer could tell that Bell had been beaten, but Bell denied it and claimed that he had "fallen down the stairs" earlier. Since he didn't want to press charges, she called him a cab and stayed with him until he left.

Bell sought medical treatment the next morning, then went into hiding for several days. He filed a formal complaint against Suge with the police, and later filed a lawsuit which resulted in a settlement of over half a million dollars.

Back in Atlanta, Christmas gave Chris and Vee another chance to revive Platinum House. A quartet of New York rappers called Onyx booked the club to celebrate the successful release of their album, "All We Got Is Us," which produced a hit single called "Slam." After their concert, the group and several hundred fans and well-wishers crammed into the club.

When the deejay put on "Slam," most of the youngsters in the club started slam dancing, and someone accidentally spilled a drink on Jay-D's Versace suit. I swear, it seemed like Jay-D hadn't taken off that damn suit since he bought it. Every time I saw him he had it on. You just don't spill stuff on a man that crazy about a suit.

Jay-D grabbed a thick champagne bottle and hit a man in Onyx's entourage over the head with it. As blood trickled down the dude's face, Jay-D started yelling to the top of his lungs that "all that East Coast slam dancing shit goes downstairs! We some West Coast players up here."

The ruckus forced everyone in the club to stare upstairs, and the music suddenly stopped. The minute all those gangsters in the club recognized that the gauntlet had been thrown down, they pounced on Jay-D and whipped him like he was a pit bull biting somebody's baby.

That was the last time the Platinum Club hosted a major event that didn't end early. As a result, the club really fell on hard times. Nobody's gonna pay good money to do the Cinderella Hustle ("be home by midnight"), so the parties drifted to other clubs in Midtown. After closing for renovations and remodeling, it reopened as the Platinum House Club and Café. For me, the whole point in working there was gone. Almost no one who could help me with my budding music career came to the club anymore, and I began to think that I would have to leave Atlanta to get my career off the ground. Since I was an East Coast transplant, leaving was no big deal.

I was fifteen years old when I arrived in Atlanta by train in 1986 to live with my father. Before that, I lived with my mother and siblings in Mississippi, and before that we lived in New Jersey. My parents, Kenneth and Lillie Curry, separated in 1983. Dad remained in New Jersey until early 1986, and he then relocated to Atlanta. After pleading with Mom off and on during their separation, he finally convinced her to give him one more chance. She sent me to live with him first to kind of check out the situation, I guess.

Mom was eager to hear my assessment of the new and improved Kenneth Curry and of the house, but I couldn't bear telling her the truth. Dad was prone to exaggeration. His description was nowhere near accurate. He told her that it was a nice size place that needed a little work, but that's like saying that comedian Bruce Bruce is a little overweight. It was a small bungalow on Washington Road in East

Point, and it was about to collapse. What it really needed was demolition and rebuilding. Luckily for us, Dad was a master carpenter.

His marriage to my mother was his second. His first wife was Johnnie Richardson, a vocalist who scored several R&B hits in the mid-1950s with Joe Rivers. The duo, called "Johnnie and Joe," was formed and promoted by Johnnie's mother, the illustrious Zelma "Zell" Sanders. Sanders was one of the first black women in America to own a record label, J&S Records.

Zell wrote a number of hits for Baby Washington and the Hearts. At first she had trouble distributing her records, but once Leonard Chess of Chess Records heard a couple of them, he personally showed up at Zell's door in Harlem to cut a distribution deal. Johnnie and Joe's first big hit, "Over the River, Across the Mountain," rose to number three on Billboard's R&B list in January 1957 after getting heavy airplay on Hal Jackson's syndicated radio show and play on Dick Clark's "American Bandstand."

That was a pretty amazing feat because America was still segregated and white radio stations rarely played music by black singers, known as "race records." Instead, they would wait until a white singer did a cover of the song. Pat Boone made a career of doing covers of black hits, for example, and some of Elvis Presley's biggest hits were written by a black man, Otis Blackwell.

Dad was also a professional singer during that period. That's how he met Johnnie. After first trying to make it as a solo artist, Dad teamed up with a white friend of his. They were probably one of the first integrated rock 'n' roll acts in America. After a promising start, however, their gigs dried up.

Dad and Johnnie produced four children – Robin, Adrian, Todd, and Diane – but no hit records, unfortunately. It ended after a few years because Johnnie was preoccupied with her recording career. Despite the breakup, Johnnie and Dad remained close friends. In fact, she and Mom were such good friends that everybody thought they were sisters.

Johnnie continued chasing the elusive limelight, but more and more of her tour dates were on the "chitlin' circuit." Even though Dad stopped performing full time, he still took occasional gigs at local clubs. After a while, he noticed that certain women would show up no matter where he performed, making them his first groupies.

Maybe that's why he and my mother had so much trouble staying together. Mom had two children – Wilbert and Debbie – from her previous relationships when they met. After they married, they had three children: Monte, Tina, and then me. We moved from New York to Teaneck, New Jersey when I was three. The tenth addition came in 1979 when I was eight years old; my five-year-old cousin Damon Sullivan joined the brood.

Our home in Teaneck was a shack made of boards and sheet metal. It was embarrassing to live there at first, but when Dad finished remodeling the place, it was the nicest house within a nine-block radius.

CHAPTER 4

Movin' On Up

For my father and many black New Yorkers in the 1970s, moving to Teaneck was the Jeffersonian Dream (as in George Jefferson). Kenneth Curry wasn't a native New Yorker. He was born in Clermont, a small town near Orlando. Grandpa took him to New York after Grandma threw Granddad out of the house. The reasons for the bitter break-up are part of our family's lore.

When Grandma was a young' un, black women were unable to have hospital births because there were no hospitals for blacks in Clermont. Other black women would come to your home to assist in childbirth. The midwives did what they could, and the Lord took care of the rest.

Upon giving birth to twins, she nursed them in the bed that she shared with my granddad. One night, she was awakened by something cold against her skin; the twin who was born sickly was dead. Grandma was still very ill and sore and was unable to move around too much. She asked Granddad to take the dead child from the bed.

He got out of bed, stood up, and then turned around to face Grandma but averted eye contact. "I can't," he said. "I can't do it."

"Well, I sure as hell can't! You know I'm not supposed to get out of bed. You're gonna have to move the baby, Honey. Please."

But Granddad was paralyzed with fear. He kept saying that touching the dead baby would bring on a curse. Grandma finally gave up. She cried and whimpered as she cradled the cold child all night.

The next day, she mustered enough strength to remove the baby girl from the bed and prepared her for burial. She cursed Granddad and she cursed him some more, and when she was finished cursing, she told him to pack his things and get out.

So Dad and Granddad moved to New York City. That was so long ago that some black New Yorkers still earned a living picking those big juicy apples. Even though he hated it, Dad picked apples with his father for seven or eight years. After Grandpa died, Dad vowed to never go near an apple orchard again in his life.

That was work for a country boy as far as he was concerned, so he found work as a cab driver, or hack. He also started doing odd jobs like home remodeling, at which he became a master. Music was his passion and home remodeling was his forte, but hacking changed his life because he met so many movers and shakers.

The nice thing about being a hacker in "the city that never sleeps" is that there's always a fare to be had. New York was overflowing with the biggest names in jazz, blues, R&B and a new type of music called rock 'n' roll. All Dad had to do to make good money was to keep circling the nightclubs. He had fares from any number of celebrities, and their tales of the high life whet his whistle.

Movin' On Up

   As R&B music skyrocketed, nightclubs discovered that they had to offer something more than music in a jukebox to keep the house full, so some owners introduced "go-go girls." The women would wear anything from a miniskirt to nothing at all, depending on the club, and they typically danced in adult-size "birdcages."

   Since he already drove a cab part-time and was always hanging out at clubs, he ended up chauffeuring a lot of go-go girls. Basically, he used the cab to get them back and forth to the clubs, and to drive some of them to their "dates" after work. Several trusted him to keep them safe while they were on these dates. A hustler was born.

   He opened a small office on 55th Street in New York to advertise his services as a dance manager and recording artist. As business improved, he stopped driving a cab and in 1969 bought a brand new Lincoln Continental with "suicide doors." Needless to say, every go-go dancer in town wanted to be his client.

   By the early 1970s, Dad was rolling in dough. Although he put his dream of a recording contract on the back burner, he spent a lot of money trying to promote himself as a singer, which meant buying recording equipment but also buying flashy clothes to look the part of an entertainer. We loved to hear Dad sing. He had a smooth baritone voice that reminded me of Arthur Prysock.

   He also opened two record shops in New York City, where I was born in July 1971. One was called Rockin' Robin, a tribute to Bobby Day's 1958 hit song and to my sister Robin. It was located at 132nd and 8th Avenue. The other shop was called Currisons, named for his sons. It was on 132nd and Madison Avenue. When record promoters and other music industry types visited to hawk their newest acts, Dad would always try to befriend them as a means of landing a record deal for himself or some of the young artists he had begun cultivating.

   He and Jerry "The Golden Voice" Bledsoe, a prominent radio personality on WBLS-AM, became close friends. Bledsoe was close to the much envied and imitated Frankie Crocker, and both played major roles in creating black music's superstars of that era. That was in the days before playlists, which have nearly regimented jazz and blues out of existence.

I learned a little bit about hustling just by watching my old man. For example, I noticed that whenever he wanted Mom's approval for something that costs a lot of money, he would bring it up while friends or relatives were present. If she said no, they would tease her about being cheap or tell her that she lacked business savvy. She usually relented to the pressure.

So I started running a similar game on Dad. Whenever I wanted something, I would wait until he was around his friends or business associates. Once he realized what I was doing, he got a little hot under the collar and told me to quit asking him for money in their presence. "You have to wake up early in the morning to fool me," he said.

I had to change tactics. I wanted these cool roller skates that all the other kids had but that Dad refused to buy me because they were too expensive. Whenever I knew Dad was chilling on the front porch, I would round up my friends and tell them to skate by my house. One by one, they would skate past him. Then I would skate past him wearing a sneaker on one foot and a borrowed skate on the other.

"Mark," he said one day after I skated past him and then headed back toward the playground, "Come in here for a minute."

He told me and my brother to get in the car. Then he took us to the sporting goods store and bought us the same fancy skates that the other kids had.

I used a similar tactic when he kept putting off buying me a new bike. There was this awesome bike at Bike Masters on Palisades in Englewood that I wanted for my birthday. A few days before the big day, Mom and I were riding with Dad in his truck. He had a huge stack of cash in the glove compartment. He had been promising all year to get me a bike for my birthday, but I knew that there was no way he would get me a custom-made one, and that's all they sold at Bike Masters. I *had* to have that bike.

I went into the shop month after month, telling the proprietor exactly what kind of bike I wanted for my birthday. He said that it would be ready as soon as I showed him some cash. Whenever I mentioned Bike Masters, Dad would tell me that it was out of the question because he couldn't afford it.

As Mom drove the truck and Dad fiddled with the cash, I said: "Daddy, you promised to buy me any bike I wanted for my birthday."

"I know, son," he said. "But I meant a regular bike and you picked the most expensive bike in the country. I can't afford to buy that expensive bike you're talking about unless you wanna go hungry for a while. We have too many bills right now."

Maybe my mother sensed what I was doing, or maybe she just wanted to pay Dad back for putting her on the spot so many times. She turned on her seductive smile and said: "Some of those bills can wait. You shouldn't make promises to the kids if you know you can't keep them."

She stuck him good with that comment. He told her to turn the car around and go to Bike Masters. The owner smiled broadly at me as I entered the store with Mom and Pop. He greeted them and told them how I had been coming into his store for months describing my dream bike.

My father smiled at me as if to acknowledge that I had hustled a hustler. "What kind of bike – "

"I want the burgundy scorpion body with the gold Araya rims, the gold three-piece sprocket set and gooseneck to match," I blurted out before he could even finish asking. He stroked the wad of cash in his pocket like it was a pet that had to be given up.

Once the bike maker finished my order and had Dad sign it, Dad ordered another one in blue for my brother Monte, a red Mongoose for Damon, a ten-speed for one sister and a training wheel bike for another. While the average regular bike costs about fifty dollars then, my bike alone cost $330. Dad spent over $1,000 that day on bikes.

Less than a month later, someone stole my brother's blue bike. Monte didn't tell anyone, but my father spent so much money for it that he immediately noticed that it was gone. When asked about the bike, Monte confessed that bullies on the basketball court at Tyrone Park had stolen it.

Some of the meanest kids at Teaneck High School hung out at Tyrone Park. We're talking about hard-core thugs. They'd beat up people just because they didn't think someone was cool enough to be at the school. So when Dad walked over to a bunch of them, I started praying for him not to start yelling because I had visions of him getting killed. He walked right into the middle of the guys on the court. They stopped playing and looked at him, but no one said a word to him.

"My boy's bike was stolen," he began. "I don't know who stole it, but I do know this. That bike had better be in my backyard by the time I wake up in the morning." He turned around and marched off with us following proudly beside him.

The next morning, my brother and I got up early to keep a vigil on the backyard. Shortly before dawn, we saw two of the boys from the basketball court climb the fence and drop the bike into the backyard.

Later that day, I overheard some of my neighbors laughing and talking about the incident.

"Them damn fools should have known not to mess with Curry," several of them said.

That's when I realized that my father struck fear in a lot of people, and that fear usually equaled respect. But I also soon discovered that other people struck fear in my father. The incident involved one of our neighbors and one of Dad's business associates.

The Diggs family lived on Carleton Terrace, about a mile from our home at 745 Intervale Road. The father, Wesley R. Diggs, owned the Diggs Den, the Yardbird Suite and two other bars in addition to a gift shop in Harlem. He and his wife Jean had five children. Like my mother, Jean Diggs was a full-time homemaker. Mr. Wesley insisted that she refrain from working just as my father insisted that my mother not work. However, Ms. Diggs was allowed to become an Avon representative.

One Sunday a few weeks before Christmas in 1975, Mr. Diggs came home after closing his businesses in Harlem and discovered that his entire family had been slaughtered. His wife, who had been shot in the back of the head and in her chest, was found in the finished basement. His seventeen-year-old daughter, Audrey, was found on her bedroom floor. She had been shot five times at close range with a .22-caliber rifle. Sixteen-year-old Allison was found in her bedroom with similar wounds from the same type of weapon. Twelve-year-old Wesley Jr. and five-year-old Roger were found in another upstairs bedroom. Like their mother and sisters, they had been shot in the back of the head with a .22-caliber rifle.

Police were baffled because there was no sign of forced entry, and because Audrey had been shot twice as many times as the other children. None of the victims had been molested, there were no signs of a struggle, and robbery clearly was not a motive.

Five days later, Stanley Morgan, another bar owner who was known to associate with Mr. Diggs, was found dead in his Shalimar Lounge bar in New Rochelle. Police said that Morgan was a major heroin trafficker in Harlem, and that Mr. Diggs had a close relative who was a known drug dealer and who happened to worked for Morgan. The Shalimar Lounge was less than a mile from Diggs Den. And like the Diggs family, Morgan was killed by a .22 caliber rifle weapon. Police had evidence that Morgan was killed by two men, each of them armed with a .22 caliber rifle gun, and a subsequent police investigation determined that two different .22 caliber rifle weapons were used in the Diggs murders.

A week before Christmas, police discovered that Mr. Diggs was heavily in debt, and that he was paying $1,000 a week on a loan of questionable origins. They speculated that he had fallen behind in payments or that his relative had double-crossed drug dealers and that someone killed the Diggs family as a result.

Although police denied that Mr. Diggs was a suspect after he passed a polygraph test, many in the community became suspicious of him. He sold his house and moved to New York. But he was still unable to put his life back together.

More than two years later, Mr. Diggs told a friend that he couldn't date because women always asked him if he had ever been married before, and he was unable to lie about it. He would end up telling his date about the execution of his family, the woman would start to look at him fearfully, and he would never see her again. He gradually sank into a deep depression and took his own life.

The murders of the Diggs family produced a few leads early on, but remains unsolved to this day. Although police believed that a trio of contract killers operating in the neighborhood was responsible for all of the murders, that was of little consolation to small business owners like my father. When two men came into his restaurant brandishing rifles during a robbery shortly after the Diggs case, Dad closed shop a few days later and then put it up for sale. He also closed his office and record shops in Harlem.

CHAPTER 5

Hard Times

Despite the brutal murder of the Diggs family and the occasional arrest of neighbors who walked on the wrong side of the law, Teaneck was a wonderful place to live. It was home to Millie Jackson, Ben E. King, and the Isley Brothers, who started their "T-Neck" recording label there in 1964.

My brother used to date Ronald Isley's daughter Tina, and my first "girlfriend" was Mia Ali, Muhammad Ali's daughter. She was the first girl I ever kissed. Her family lived about three blocks from us, and we both attended Benjamin Franklin Junior High.

I was part of a break dancing crew called "The Breaking Sensations." We were good; hell, we were awesome. We'd enter almost every local talent show and contest and win. In those days, you were pretty cool if you knew how to break dance. If you didn't, you were considered lame. Our crew was like a gang or something from the movie "Grease." We settled our differences through break dancing. Despite my badge of coolness, I was attracting more flies than girls. Mia had to educate me about the link between personal hygiene and attracting the babes.

"You're a nice boy," Mia said, "but your clothes are always wrinkled – like they just came out of the dryer or like you slept in them or something." When she said that, my eyes opened wide like I'd just seen a ghost. "Damn, is it that obvious?" I wondered to myself before noticing just how apparent it was.

"And you need to brush your hair. You always have so much lint in it," she said.

I slept in my clothes most nights to save time getting ready for school the next day. I also brushed my teeth and combed my hair just before going to bed, thinking that both would still be as fresh as sunrise. I guess I should have been embarrassed because my girlfriend criticized my personal hygiene, but I wasn't. She taught me so much, even about the importance of color-coordinating my clothes. She was a true friend. It wasn't until she schooled me that I noticed how dapper Dad looked all the time. Talk about a sharp-dressed man.

In addition to his record stores, Dad once owned a small recording studio and cabinet shop on Palisades Avenue in Englewood. The studio attracted the young and the old, the rich and the poor, and people from all walks of life who were looking for that big break. The first rap group that Dad worked with was TC and the Dangerous 3 out of Spring Valley, New York. He also recorded Kid Capri and the Five Lords of Funk. Neither act ever made it big, but Kid Capri went on to success as a deejay on "Def Jam Comedy" and the movies.

Many of his studio guests visited our home. I would spend hours watching Dad interact with them, negotiating studio rates, discussing promotional ideas, you name it. Sometimes after the guests left, he would tell me why he said or did a certain thing, so I learned a lot from the old man about business strategy and psychology. He made me feel early on that I was a star. I was proud of him, and I dreamed of making him proud of me someday by becoming an entertainer, the dream that got away from him.

But Dad, like a lot of black people enjoying "ghetto fabulous" lives, had a dark side. When I was in junior high school, kids would run up to me and accuse my father of being a hustler and a drug dealer. I thought it was only jealousy talking because I hadn't seen anything to indicate that he wasn't simply and innovative, hard-working businessman.

In fact, when he closed his record shops, he used the money to convert an old gas station in Bergenfield into a combined record store and restaurant called Inter-City. My older siblings worked there. It was next to one of the most popular skating rinks in the tri-state area, so he made good money and paid his employees well. I had never seen anything shady at the shop, and the police never visited the shop or our home to interview or arrest him for anything.

Still, with so many friends telling me the same thing, I finally gathered the courage to confront my parents about the rumors. They denied it, as I had expected and hoped. They both expressed outrage that someone would say that about him.

Once those seeds were planted, however, questions about my father grew in my mind. I started to look at the people who visited our home and the shop differently as I read stories and saw on television how underworld types behave and dress. It finally occurred to me that he was probably doing something that wasn't kosher, but I was too young to sort through all the smoke and mirrors.

I gradually realized that some of the people whom I thought were just flashy dressers were in fact hustlers, gigolos and chili pimps. And I noticed that Dad was having trouble sleeping at night. I'd hear him walking around the house or making noise in the kitchen at all times of the night. I'd see him peeping out the windows sometimes when I ventured downstairs, like he was standing guard over his family. That scared me because it reminded me of the Diggs family.

A few months after I quizzed them, my parents started having major marital problems. At first I thought that my interrogating them was the source. As it happens, Mom learned from her friends that Dad was having an extramarital affair on the other side of town, and that he had fathered several children with the woman. All of her children had the Curry surname. Mom stopped sleeping with him, turning the bedroom into a war zone.

"Sleeping with your momma is like sleeping with a block of ice," he'd say in front of us.

"I don't want you putting your lips on me," Mom would shoot back. "I don't know where they've been."

They were having an explosive argument one evening when my father called all of us into their bedroom. He was holding his .38-caliber pistol and he had his index finger on the trigger. Mom was yelling and screaming at him, and Dad kept telling her to be quiet because one of his employees was downstairs in the living room waiting on him.

"I don't give a damn who's downstairs!" Mom shouted. "This is my house and I'll talk as loud as I want."

"Kenny," the man downstairs yelled, "I'll talk to you later. I have another appointment." As he closed the door, I could see my father turn red from embarrassment.

Exasperated, Dad pointed the gun at Mom and said, "If you don't stop talking, I'm going to put a bullet right through your goddamn head!"

"Do it, muthafucka!" Mom dared him. "You so big and bad, do it."

"Oh, I'll do it," he replied. "And I'll kill these kids, too. Which one do you want to see die first?"

Mom wasn't buying his wolf tickets. "Shoot me, muthafucka," she kept saying, "shoot me if you so goddamn big and bad."

By now, we were panicking. "Please, Momma, be quiet," I pleaded along with my sisters and brothers. "Daddy, please put your gun away."

When Dad saw how badly he was frightening us, he bowed his head in shame, laid the gun on the bed and walked out of the room. One of my brothers picked up the gun and foolishly looked into the chamber.

"Ain't no bullets even in there," he said.

Dad overheard him. He came back into the room and faced my brother who was holding the gun. "Since you're so smart, put the bullets in the gun and shoot me." My brother quickly placed the gun back on the bed and walked away from him and towards us.

Dad left the house that night and didn't return until the next morning. When he walked into the kitchen and saw Mom crying, he must have known that his crazy talk about killing us was unforgivable and that their marriage was over.

Over the next few months, his life started crumbling. The Internal Revenue Service got after him, and shortly after that his businesses crashed. Mom secretly started moving things out of the house and shipping them down South in preparation for leaving the marriage.

While Dad was away one day in the fall of 1983, Mom took us by train to Bear Town in McComb, Mississippi, where she grew up. From the moment she got there, though, our lives became a constant struggle. We moved into the home of Fannie May Gayden, a relative who raised my mother and my oldest brother, Wilbert.

I learned about musicians on my mother's side of the family after we settled in. For those familiar with gospel music, my cousins were members of the Sensational Williams Brothers and the Jackson Southernaires. Learning about them piqued my interest in religion, so I began reading the Bible.

Mom had a tough time finding work because she had been a housewife all of her life and had no marketable skills. Desperate for income, she found work as a cashier at a local grocery store. It was chump change, and she could never make ends meet.

Since Mom was having such a hard time feeding us, I went to stay with Wilbert, who lived twenty miles away on a farm in Tylertown, Mississippi. Living in the boondocks gave me time to reflect. Life moved so fast in Teaneck that there was little time to do that. I fed the pigs, fished, picked crops from the fields and fruit from the vine and trees. I even broke in my own horse. Unlike Teaneck, where you could always find somewhere to hang out, people lived so far apart in Tylertown that there were very few ways of escaping the drudgery of country living.

Other than going to school, the only guaranteed means of getting to know girls was to attend church. I joined a local church and tried to spend as much of my weekends there as possible. I also tried to attend revivals, no matter whose church was conducting it, because there was always plenty of down home cooking and fine Southern girls.

After I was baptized, I prayed constantly to God to reunite my parents. I missed my father terribly despite his occasionally abusive ways, and Mom seemed so sad now.

We soon learned that Dad had left his girlfriend in Teaneck and moved to Atlanta to make a fresh start. After discovering where we were, he started calling to check up on us. He kept promising to visit and to send money to help Mom, but neither promise was kept. Mom was so deep in the hole that by the time Dad did send something, she had to spend it all on clothing or bills.

He made things worse on his first visit by bringing us a dog that we left behind in Teaneck. He was shocked by how destitute we were and started calling frequently, always begging Mom to take him back. He told her about the "great deal" that he landed on a piece of property in Atlanta.

"It's nice, Dad, real nice," I lied when he asked my opinion about the place. What it really needed was demolition and rebuilding. Kids would snicker at us when they passed by and saw me pulling weeds or mowing the lawn.

"It may not look like much now," he kept telling me. "But wait until I'm finished.

Once again, Dad's skill as a carpenter and handyman made the house blossom. I spent several months by his side learning home remodeling, everything from framing a room to plumbing to the basics of electrical installation. After we got the house in livable condition, the rest of my family joined us.

I enrolled at Lakeshore High in Southwest Atlanta in August 1986. I was a decent student in the first two years, but something deep within me had come undone as my junior year began. By the time the bell rang for first period, my body was in the classroom but my mind had wandered down the hall and through the exit doors, transporting me back home where I spent every spare minute trying to compose songs.

Sometimes I was writing lyrics on the notebook pages when I should have been jotting down notes from the history lecture. By the time winter break arrived, I was consumed by music. I stayed up so late at night that I found myself getting up for school less and less, much to my parent's dismay.

I met several people in school who also had dreams of making music their career. None of us realized it then, but Atlanta was slowly becoming the new mecca for black music. One of my classmates at Lakeshore was a dude named Dallas Austin. He moved to Atlanta from Columbus, Georgia when I was in my junior year, and quickly established a reputation as a music maven. But Austin had such quixotic goals for someone with so few connections that I assumed that he would ultimately burn out and abandon them.

We bumped into each other one day at the mall and started chatting about our shared passion. I told him that I was working on a few songs in my spare time, but that I had to work a nine-to-five to help keep food on the table.

"If you work with me on your music," he said, "I might be able to help you." I almost laughed in his face because I'm thinking that here's this cat who's my age with no hit record notches on his belt as far as I knew, standing here talking to me like he's the new Berry Gordy and I'm some kinda naïve kid. So I smiled at him and said something like, "Yeah, okay. I may just take you up on that."

When I mentioned the incident several weeks later to some friends, they told me that Austin had dropped out of school and was working with a former member of the singing group called Klymaxx. I still wasn't impressed. I knew that he was talented (he played multiple instruments, including piano, drums, and guitar), but I wasn't convinced that he would strike gold any quicker than I because he seemed to spread himself too thin. Every time I talked to him he was working with another artist but never had anything solid. Klymaxx's hot streak had already come and gone by then. To my surprise, Austin hooked up Klymaxx vocalist Joyce "Finderella" Irby and rapper Doug E. Fresh a few years later to produce his first hit record, "Hey Mr. DJ."

Austin finally had my attention, but now he was so busy that it was impossible to get him on the phone. In 1990, he produced a song called "I Will Always Love You," and several other hits for Troop, a singing group on the Atlantic label. When I heard that he had moved to Los Angeles to work for Motown, I remembered the encounter at the mall when I jokingly compared him to Gordy.

His first success at Motown was with a group of preteens who called themselves "Another Badd Creation. Their song "Aisha" went straight to the top of Billboard in 1991. From there, his career went into warp speed. In short order, Austin penned hits for Boyz II Men, Monica, and the Atlanta-based group called 112 (pronounced "one-twelve" in honor of a popular nightclub in Midtown). He later produced the movie, "Drumline."

About the same time in my junior year that I met Austin, I met a sister named Tionne Watkins. All the popular kids had nicknames, so everybody called her "T-Boz." We'd talk on the phone, mainly about our ambitions. At first she tried modeling, but gave up on it after too much negative feedback. Then she tried being a beautician. When that fell through, she joined a singing group. That's when I started having trouble reaching her. It seemed that every time I called her, she was rehearsing. They called themselves "Second Nature." I heard them once, and honestly, I concluded that all the rehearsing in the world wouldn't improve their sound.

Less than a year later, the group changed its lineup and renamed itself TLC. Austin ended up producing the group's biggest hits after they signed with LaFace Records in 1991, and he also produced a son with group member Rozonda "Chili" Thomas.

Another high school student in Atlanta whose career began in his freshman year at North Clayton High was Jermaine Dupri. When he was 12 years old, he worked as a breakdancer with Whodini and Run DMC. He used to ride around town his father's Chevy Astro van filled with boxes of cassette tapes of various artists with whom he collaborated. He had his own studio and his own record label, So So Def. He was only 14 when he produced the first album for the female trio, "Silk Times Leather." The album didn't fare well, but it brought Dupri to the attention of Geffen Records. In 1992, he produced his first platinum-selling album for these two kids called Kriss Kross.

Derek Stephens was yet another cat I got to know in school. Although he lived among the homeless, crack heads, and teenage mothers in the Red Oak housing projects in College Park, Stephens had the heart of a winner. He formed a dance troupe called the Federal Dance Committee that was in constant demand to perform in Atlanta. He was known as "Devyne the Dancer" because of his incredible choreographic skills.

He also formed a rap group call DeVyne and 90MPH, one of the first groups signed to LaFace Records by LA Reid and Babyface. They mimicked MC Hammer's style too closely, however, and internal bickering led to the group's demise before the first album was even finished. Thus, they also became one of the first groups dropped by LaFace.

Even though his group self-destructed, Stephens was hired as a choreographer for the label. His creativity was soon evident in music videos by Michael Jackson, Usher, TLC, and Mary J. Blige, among others. He also worked extensively with Puff and his artists. Rather than squander his millions, Stephens started his own record label and artist development company. After founding Upfront Records in the early 1990s, he signed an unknown artist who had just been dumped by Elektra. From Senegal, the dude's real name is Aliaune Badara Akon Thiam, but he's now known as Akon.

CHAPTER 6

The Rim Shop

While Austin and Stephens were finding stardom, I was finding stagnation. Lakeshore merged with Westwood High School to become Westlake in my senior year, and anyone who's been through that experience in a big city can tell you horror stories that mergers cause. Class scheduling problems, social cliques, and turf wars were out of control. To make matters worse, I felt this overwhelming urge to follow Austin's lead and just drop out to pursue music on a full-time basis.

In September 1987, an old friend of mine nicknamed Vee stopped by Lakeshore to visit me and some other former buddies. He left with his mom two years earlier and moved to Minnesota. His outfit made me do a double take because he was wearing very expensive sneakers and clothing. Then he pulled a huge wad of bills out of his right front pocket. He flashed it and we could see that there was nothing there smaller than a twenty.

Just like Mr. Robinson in the "The Graduate" told the young cat dating his daughter that the key to future prosperity rested in the word "plastic," Vee told us that the quickest way to a wad of cash like his could be summed up in one word: crack.

A few weeks later, a guy named Bernard came into the jewelry store. He paid for his rings with bills from a roll of money as thick as the one Vee had shown us. When my friend Loc asked him how he could get his own roll like that, Bernard told him that he could start selling crack cocaine for him. In a matter of days, Loc was making a profit, so I asked Loc to get me into the game. He gave me a sack of crack to sell at Club Candlewood, an apartment complex close to my house on Washington Road.

For some reason, I had a hell of a time making sales. It would take me damn near a whole day to clear a twenty-dollar profit. Part of my problem was that crackheads shop with a familiar face first, and another part was that I started negotiating with them, which was a major mistake. This girl whom I knew asked me to give her a couple of rocks on credit until later that evening. She gave me her address book as collateral. I figured that was cool because she probably had the phone numbers of all of her suppliers in it.

I didn't examine the book closely until later. It was a dud. Two weeks later, I was still stuck with a useless address book and in debt to Loc for the price of two rocks. I didn't see that girl again for months. That was the last time I ever trusted anyone hooked on drugs. I let them know that my business was strictly cash and carry: no negotiating, no bartering, and no credit. Profits increased dramatically once I started thinking and acting like a true hustler.

In fact, things were going very well until I came home from school one afternoon and found my sister's boyfriend in my room. He was standing in front of my dresser as I opened the door, holding my sack of crack in his hand.

"Stop selling this shit or I'll tell your momma," he threatened. Mom was working part-time at as a cashier at a gas station. Dad probably wouldn't have said much if Bobby told him, but it would have broken my mother's heart if she found out what I was doing. I stopped selling drugs that same day, and when Mom came home from work that night, I asked her if she could help me get a job at the gas station. She said yes. The next day I returned the sack to Loc and told him that I was quitting because I wasn't making enough money, so I was going legit.

I started out as a stock clerk and maintenance man, but the boss man let me work as a cashier on weekends. Sometimes I would swipe some of the candy from stock and sell it at school. Then I started taking nickels or dimes from many of my sales. Little did I know that book-keepers and hidden cameras were on to me. Boss man gave me the option of quitting or being arrested. One of the easiest decisions I ever made.

Shortly after I got fired, I ended up getting suspended, unfairly I thought. I remember the day the principal called me into her office. I told her that she was wrongfully accusing me, but she wouldn't listen. I warned her that if she suspended me, I would not come back. She did, so I didn't. My parents were not happy about that, especially Dad. He recounted his own frustrating attempts to become an entertainer, and noted how Johnnie's career took a nosedive even after several hit records.

She was traveling around doing oldies shows by the early 1980s but her main source of income was from her Johnnie-On-the-Spot ambulance service. Founded in 1985, Johnnie had two vans outfitted exclusively for transporting wheelchair-bound clients. People called her home phone number to get door-to-door service.

"Since you're too damn smart for school," he said sternly, "you can find a job and start paying your own way in life."

"Okay," I replied with mock confidence. "No problem. I can get a job at the mall."

I started hanging out at a jewelry store in the Greenbrier Mall because I knew the guy named Steve who owned the place. His father had passed recently and had willed the store to his only son. Although his father primarily sold jewelry, Steve quickly discovered that he was making a fortune selling four-finger and five-finger rings, and that the second hottest item was the unique graffiti-type Tee-shirts which were designed while the customer waited. Steve hired my brother Monte, my friend Zack White, and another dude to draw anything the customer wanted on a shirt as long as it wasn't something that would bring the cops into the shop.

It was fascinating listening to people describe what they wanted on the shirts and then seeing them look surprised when the artists improved upon what the customer envisioned. I wanted to try my hand at it, but unfortunately, I couldn't draw a lick. They were attracting bevies of beautiful girls to the store while working their magic before the large plate-glass window. Since I couldn't join them but I still wanted to be at the mall with them, I settled for a job at Chick-Fil-a in the food court. I had applied for a cashier position but the only opening they had was for a janitor. I was sliding around as I tried to mop the greasy floors in the back kitchen.

After the first shift ended, I knew that I would have to quit if I didn't get another assignment. I went to the manager at the beginning of my shift the next afternoon and requested another job. The manager agreed. She assigned me to buttering and toasting buns on the butter wheel. Midway through the shift, the manager asked if I would assist in cleaning the dining area after my break.

"Sure," I said. I left for my break, went to the jewelry store to watch my brother design shirts, and never went back to the restaurant, not even to pick up my paycheck for one and one-half days of grunt work.

I guess my parents sensed that I was heading for trouble because Dad started putting a lot of pressure on me to find a better job, something with career possibilities. He urged me to consider construction work, but when I was too slow to get the hint, he drafted me into his renovation business.

He worked me hard, which I really didn't mind until he started messing with my money. Every payday, he'd find a new way to avoid paying me in full. He would offer to buy me lunch during the week, and then deduct it from my pay without even asking me.

He started charging me rent, again deducting it from my pay the first time without telling me that he intended to do so. The last straw was the week that he deducted rent and lunch fees from my check, and then charged me for riding to work with him in his van! I had less than fifty dollars after all the petty charges, and I began to feel like God's stepchild.

Maybe he was trying to make working conditions so bad for me that I would go back to school. If that was his message, it missed the target. We were having heated arguments over the way he was paying me, and I rarely won. Consequently, we drifted apart.

So did he and Mom for the umpteenth time. They were having constant disagreements and were swearing at each other like sailors. Mom, it turned out, had caught Dad making mysterious telephone calls at odd hours of the night. He'd be smiling and grinning and saying things which she knew that a man only says to a lover, and then he would get that guilty look on his face when he realized that she knew he was talking to another woman.

When the phone bill arrived, she saw that he had placed a lot of calls to the woman who had borne his children in New Jersey. In early 1990, Mom packed his bags one day while he was at work and placed them by the front door. When he came home, he knew what time it was. He said his goodbyes to us and headed back to New Jersey.

I guess that just because God answers a prayer doesn't mean that that's His final answer, and it may not be your final prayer on the subject. Sometimes when people have a prayer answered and see the can of worms that it opens up, they get right back down on their knees and pray for just the opposite. That's what I had done. I had prayed for my father to come back home and he did.

I had forgotten in his absence how bad things were between the two of them, but it all came rushing back after he was home for a few months. When I saw how miserable Mom was, I wished that Dad would just go away. I didn't pray on it, at least not directly, but the truth is that a wish is nothing but another kind of prayer. The next thing I know, God had answered my prayers again; Dad was gone and Mom was smiling again.

I had secretly started applying for jobs elsewhere after Dad started stiffing my paycheck, and I was hired by Eastern Airlines as a ramp agent the week after he returned to New Jersey. I loaded luggage and bundles of mail into the underbelly of the airplanes. Within a few weeks, some of the older hands started schooling me on how to make extra money on the ramp. They showed me how easy it was to open luggage and remove valuables like cameras, watches, and what not. And they taught me how to remove new credit cards from the mail.

Drug dealers also played a game with ramp agents. They would place large amounts of cash in the same bag as their drugs. The game was to take the money in exchange for letting the dealer smuggle the drugs aboard. I was making so much extra money on the side after a while that I vowed to never leave my job. Unfortunately, Eastern Airlines went bankrupt in 1991. I knew it was too good to be true. The best job I had ever had lasted less than a year. I spent the next few years moving from job to job.

I also started hanging out among college students because a lot of my friends were attending Clark Atlanta University and Morris Brown College. I was on one campus or the other damn near every day for a while, hanging around the student center with a backpack in tow like I was between classes. Man, talk about frontin'. I was having an absolute ball – nothing but house parties, fine women, and keggers at the fraternity houses.

When things got boring on campus, many students hung out at a club called "The Warehouse," which featured live entertainment. A local group of rappers called the "East Point Chain Gang" made their debut there in 1992 and was booed offstage. Three years later, and under a different name – the Goodie Mob – the group had its first gold album and was credited with creating a new style of rap music called "Dirty South."

With so much music being created by young cats all over Atlanta, and so many of my colleagues achieving their dreams, I had an intense desire to launch my own music career. Not far from our home was a nightclub called "Club Oxygen." I started just watching people perform on Tuesday evenings, which was "open mike" night. Most of the performers were people I had seen around the neighborhood or at school or something. Few of them had star presence. If I had to categorize the talent on "open mike" night, I'd say that 60 percent were mediocre, 30 percent were terrible, and the remaining 10 percent had genuine talent.

"Open mike" night was hosted by Jazze Pha and Bone Crusher, both popular Atlanta emcees, and the house band was called "Little John and the Chronicles." Little John was Janet Jackson's drummer. There was no telling whom you'd see at "open mike" night. I saw MC Brand and Erick Sermon in there a lot. I also bumped into Too Short.

I needed eight or nine visits to Club Oxygen before I could muster enough courage to get up there in front of the microphone. Oxygen was known as a place where people went to forget about their everyday troubles, where you could dance the night away and never think twice about the mean realities waiting outside the front door. I was filled with apprehension as I approached the stage, afraid that the crowd would be turned off by lyrics which portrayed the very problems that they were there to forget about.

In my book, there's nothing better than live music. Listening to real drums, real guitars, and real horns has an effect on the body and soul that exposes the paleness of electronic imitation. The Chronicles got me fired up, and I launched into my rap with a vigor that surprised even me. One minute I felt like I was Tupac, and the next like I was Biggie, and the next like someone who could be bigger than both of them. I felt larger than life.

I knew that I had done well; I could tell by the crowd's reaction. The clapping was genuine, and some of the women looked at me like I was already a superstar. As I made my way back to my table I was stopped by this cat named Greg Taylor, whom everyone called "Gee."

"Man, was that really you? I thought that was Biggie up there doin' his thing!" He couldn't have paid me a higher compliment because Biggie was the most adulated rapper in the world at the time.

The high I received from performing that night propelled me back to Club Oxygen the next Tuesday, and the one after that, and before long it became an addiction. I lived for Tuesday night. I felt that it was only a matter of time before word reached the local record company talent scouts that a star was waiting to be signed.

However, as the weeks passed by and no one showed up with a contract, my enthusiasm started to wane. Although I still received raves from the crowd, I didn't want to grow stale on them like so many other local musicians who were no more than furniture at the places where they performed.

To avoid that hell, I stop performing. I channeled my energies into writing my own songs and looking for somewhere to record them. Maybe Gee sensed my disillusionment because a few weeks after I stopped going to Oxygen he offered me a job at The Rim Shop. Originally from Detroit, Gee and his brothers had only recently settled in Atlanta. Once the profits started rolling in, Gee moved the shop from Old National Highway to Covington Highway, then eventually to the corner of Peachtree and Ralph Mc Gill, right in the heart of downtown.

The shop couldn't have opened at a better time. Most of the videos on MTV and BET showed cars that had been "pimped" or redesigned with outrageous additions. Because of its location, the shop attracted the attention of a lot of local and national hip hop stars. Word of mouth gave the shop a national reputation, and The Rim Shop soon became a mandatory stop for major artists.

One of the regulars was MC Breed, who had a gangster hit in 1991 with "Ain't No Future in Fronting." It's a serious hip hop classic. Since Breed was from Detroit and nearly everybody who worked in the shop was from Detroit, Breed came to the shop almost every day after he moved to Atlanta in 1993. In fact, MC Breed was the person who introduced me to Jazze Pha. Jazze used to stay with Breed and produce out of Breed's home studio in Marietta. He had blonde hair and two

big hoop earrings in either ear, reminding you of Mr. Clean. Jazze's the son of James Alexander of the Bar Kays.

Too Short moved from Oakland to Atlanta in 1993 and he, too, became a regular at the shop. People seemed to really appreciate him here. He opened up Dangerous Music record label offices in the West End of Atlanta.

Hip hop legend Erick Sermon moved to Atlanta in 1992. Sermon is the "E" of EPMD. The initials stood for "Erick and Parrish Making Dollars." Parrish Smith was the other member of the duo. In December 1991, rumor had it that Sermon paid $5,000 to thugs for breaking into Parrish's home. Sermon was supposedly upset about how Smith was running their business. After police caught one of the burglars, he claimed that Sermon was the mastermind. Sermon and Smith were on a national tour at the time, which lasted for almost a year. Police were hassling Sermon so much that he left everything he owned in New York and moved to Atlanta. The only thing he had when he arrived was the keyboard he used during the tour. Luckily for him, Dallas Austin agreed to support him financially until he got back on his feet.

Gee let Sermon live in the basement of The Rim Shop. Since he was always there, people got the impression that Sermon owned the shop, which really increased traffic and sales. Hustlers from all over came into the shop just to say that they bought rims from Sermon. Since Sermon was trying to restart his career, Gee set up a recording studio for him in the basement.

Civil rights activist Hosea Williams had an office next door to the shop. It seemed like every morning Hosea would come to work with something different damaged on his car. Despite his shortcomings, Hosea was a good man. He would stay on our cases about wasting money on unimportant things when we could be donating some to feed the hungry. We all nodded in agreement with Hosea, but the truth was that we were too focused on creating a first-rate recording studio to think much about anything else.

One of our biggest spenders was a Detroit gangster known as "Meech." His real name was Demetrius Flenory. Therein lies a tale, but for another day.

CHAPTER 7

Smitten

In late 1993, Sermon started working with Keith Murray and Reginald "Redman" Noble. Sermon and Murray produced their first collaboration in 1994, which they sold to Jive Records. Titled "The Most Beautifullest Thing in This World," the title track was a monster hit.

While helping Sermon get reestablished, Dallas Austin teamed up with L.A. Reid to create Rowdy Records in Atlanta. The label was run by Austin's brother, Claude. Initially, they had two artists signed to the label, "Shadz of Lingo" and a young rap duo called "Illegal," featuring Mally G and a cat who called himself Li'l Malik. The group's 1993 debut album, "Untold Truth," produced a single hit, a number called "We Get Buzy" which featured Sermon, Biz Markie, and Claude. Malik left Atlanta and went west, changed his moniker to Mr. Malik, and started recording music with Suge Knight's "Death Row" label. Name change or not, what he did really was illegal since Malik was still under contract with Rowdy Records. A test of wills was on.

Claude Austin, it turned out, had a congenital heart defect. He suffered from heart murmurs. Suge Knight, who had just started Death Row, wanted to meet with Claude to discuss terminating Malik's contract with Rowdy. The dispute grew volatile, so Claude reluctantly agreed to meet on Suge's own turf. No one knows the details, but Claude died of heart failure during his stay in Los Angeles.

Claude's death raised suspicions among friends because Suge had been involved in other incidents where people were threatened over contract disputes with Death Row. In 1991, for example, white rapper Vanilla Ice reported that Suge and some of his bodyguards showed up unannounced at his hotel room. Suge demanded that Ice sign over his royalties to his platinum hit single "Ice, Ice Baby," because the artist had allegedly sampled a Death Row song without permission. Ice said that he signed the contract only after Suge and his associates dangled him head first over the hotel's balcony.

A year later, Eric "Eazy-E" Wright of the hip hop group NWA filed a lawsuit against Suge and Death Row in which he claimed that Suge and his bodyguards, armed with lead pipes and baseball bats, burst into his recording studio and threatened to kill him unless he released former NWA member Dr. Dre from his recording contract with Wright. Suge was working as a bodyguard for another member of NWA at the time. After Wright destroyed the contract, Dre became the debut artist of Death Row.

Using NWA's reputation as collateral, Suge secured a distribution deal with Interscope Records. One of the first artists to work with Dr. Dre on his debut album was Calvin Broadus, better known as Snoop Dogg. Snoop Dogg was said to be Li'l Malik's cousin, and he was anxious to join Dogg at Death Row. So given how Suge dealt with other people who stood between him and his objectives, it's no wonder that rumors spread about the underlying cause of Claude Austin's sudden death.

I spent my days at The Rim Shop and my nights at Platinum House. In addition to working security, I sometimes deejayed on slow nights. One night I was checking identification when this young lady caught my eye. I was so busy staring at her that I forgot to even check her ID. I wanted to flirt with her for a minute, but you can't slow down a line of people in a hurry to get a party started or you'll cause a riot.

So I let her in and moved on to the next customer. I took a break an hour or so later and went through the club looking for her. I spotted her and her friend at a table near the front of the club.

"Hey, let me buy you a drink," I said, flashing a seductive smile.

"No, but thank you," she said.

"Okay, Miss – what's your name again?"

"Deirdre."

"Okay, Deirdre, maybe some other time, then. You all have a wonderful time."

I walked away feeling dejected but refused to let it show. I made conversation with Vee for a minute to try to impress upon her that I was more than just a doorman, that I knew people. As I made my way back to the door, I tried to devise Plan B to get Deirdre's phone number before she left.

Jay-D was in the club that night. I pointed out Deirdre and her friend to him, hoping that the friend was his type of woman. He said that any woman was his type of woman, so I told him to introduce himself to her friend and offer to buy her a drink. "Whatever you do, be sure to get her number."

Thankfully, Jay-D had more success with the friend than I had with Deirdre. The next day, Jay-D called Tracy and invited her and Deirdre out to dinner. She called Jay-D back a few minutes later and said that she and Deirdre had accepted his offer. Jay-D told them that I would be joining them.

We took them to this fancy Italian restaurant downtown. It had chandeliers, live music, and a five-star rating. I could tell they were impressed not only by the restaurant's elegance, but also because we had not taken them to the typical places that young brothers take their dates – you know, like the Red Lobster or the corner buffet.

The second part of our plan came at the conclusion of the meal. Since Jay-D's interest in Tracy was only marginal, he pretended to be broke once the check was placed on the table.

"Damn," he said, "I barely have enough money to pay for my meal." He knew that the women would not be paying, so he looked at me and asked, "How much money you got on you?"

"Don't worry, man," I said as I pulled out my wallet and let the women see a thick stack of bills. "I got it covered." I noticed that Deirdre and her friend were very impressed. I had already told them during dinner about all the celebrities I met at my "real job" at The Rim Shop. I also lied and said that I only worked at Platinum House as a favor to Vee. "He knows that I can handle any situation which might arise at the door," I said.

After placing a generous tip on the table, I tucked the payment for the meal inside the leather check case. Then I walked over and stood behind Deirdre and held her seat like the dudes do in those classic black-and-white movies. Again, I could tell that she was impressed.

Jay-D and I double-dated Deirdre and Tracy for a few weeks. My first impression was correct: I had met the woman of my dreams. It wasn't love at first sight for her, but she quickly warmed up to me. After several joint dates and kisses in dark corners, she agreed that it was time to leave our best friends at home. From that moment on, our love blossomed. We started talking about moving in together, which we did four or five months after we met.

Deirdre became my muse, my primary motivator. I could work all day at The Rim Shop and then work a shift at Platinum House and still have enough energy to stay in the studio for five hours the same evening.

The reputation of the Rim Shop and Platinum House heightened at about the same time, so what happened is that you would meet many of the same people at both. Two of the exceptions were Biggie Smalls and Tupac Shakur, both of whom I met at Platinum. Biggie was there with Puff.

Tupac, however, visited Atlanta frequently because his mother, Afeni Shakur, lived here. He would come to Platinum, take the dance floor, and dance about 30 seconds with as many different women as time permitted. Every woman in the club wanted to dance with him.

Chris and Conrad Rosser, two of my friends from my deejay days, were running their own studio in College Park at the time. It was called Bread and Butter Productions. They persuaded Tupac to visit the studio and lay down some tracks with them after they played several samples for him. As a result, Tupac ended up recording about half a dozen songs there. The most popular ones are "When I Get Free 2" and "Thug Style." Tupac had planned to include them on his "Me Against the World" compact disc, but they ended up on "R U Still Down (Remember Me)," which was released after his death.

In addition to owning half of Platinum House, Vee had also gotten into the music business. One of the first things he did after returning to Atlanta from Minnesota was to buy a home off Flake Mills Road in Decatur. He remodeled the place from top to bottom and built a state-of-the-art recording studio in the basement.

Anthony Dent, who had befriended Vee when he was in Minnesota, was one of the first people to move into Vee's home. Dent brought along his girlfriend Shelley and their baby. Even though Dent wasn't making any money, Vee told him not to worry about it. Vee was interesting in doing some rapping and hoping that Dent could school him. He told Dent to just concentrate on writing music and learning how to work the equipment. At the time, Dent didn't know a reverberator from an oscillator, a MIDI from a patchbay. But you have to give him credit. He stayed in the studio day and night, and before long, he sounded like he was born with a mixing console in his crib.

Vee also invited two budding songwriters from Detroit, Teddy Bishop and Tim Thomas, to move to Atlanta at his expense. They were as poor as church mice. Sometimes they would be so hungry that they would come by the shop and ask Vee to hurry home and fix some Hamburger Helper.

At the time, Antonio "LA" Reid and Kenneth "Babyface" Edmonds had LaFace Records in Atlanta. When Thomas and Bishop were ready to go professional, Vee introduced them to LaFace.

They made a big impression there. Reid, who had a studio in his home in Atlanta at the time, moved out and let the duo move in so they could have around-the-clock access to a personalized studio and everything they needed to live in style. It wasn't long before Reid's investment paid dividends.

Bishop and Thomas scored their first hit with "Love Affair," a single from Toni Braxton's platinum-selling debut album in 1993. The duo went their separate ways shortly thereafter, with Thomas going into gospel music and Bishop staying with neo-soul and hip hop. Bishop wrote hits for Aaliyah, Usher, Genuwine, and Whitney Houston, among others.

He also took Dent to Noontime Studios once his skills had matured. A lot of people outside of the business may not recognize his name still, but he made and revived the careers of several artists. One of Dent's earliest accomplishments was producing "Survivor" for Destiny's Child. The song debuted at Number One on Billboard's Pop chart in 2001 and was one of the biggest hits in the history of Columbia Records.

Dent was also the engineer on that song and others on the album. He also played a major role in Jay-Z's "In My Lifetime" album, the third album for 112 ("Friend of Mine" was a song he composed with Kelly Price which became a big hit), and dozens of others.

Platinum House had begun having financial problems after Big Jake died, and Chris and Vee concluded that the club was no longer viable. Vee planned to close it, renovate it, and reopen in the spring of 1996. Chris had other plans.

"I'm going back to Minnesota for a while," he said. "You're welcome to come along."

I was hesitant to go because it meant leaving my lady here in Atlanta. On the other hand, Chris convinced me that I could make some serious money fast there. That was a strong incentive for me because I wanted to buy an MPC-3000 beat machine that costs more than $2,000. I convinced myself that I would run up there with him, stay long enough to earn money for the machine, and then come back to my sweetheart in Atlanta and jumpstart my music career.

I had never been to Minnesota before, and I really wasn't looking forward to that cold-ass weather after being in Atlanta. However, I had seen my own brother and others go there for awhile and come back with money to spare. I needed something to make up for the income that I lost with the shuttering of Platinum House, and since I was short on marketable skills, Minnesota seemed to be calling my name.

People didn't know it then – hell, neither did I – but Minneapolis and other big cities in Minnesota had become havens for street gangs involved in the drug trade. The Crips, the Bloods, the Gangster Disciples, and the Latin Kings all had units there. So did racists group like the Skinheads and the Ku Klux Klan.

Chris' home was located in an ordinary pleasant middle class neighborhood, or so I thought. But within my first two hours at his house, a young kid was gunned down less than 200 feet from the doorway, and it proved to be gang-related. I rushed to the scene of the murder with Chris' brother and cousin.

As we stood there observing, the growing crowd grew angry and accused us of being involved. I damn near wet my pants because a lot of them were gang members and nearly all of them seemed to be carrying weapons. They let us leave after a minor shoving match and after we explained to their satisfaction that we were just there checking things out like everybody else.

From that moment on, I knew that this was not Mr. Rogers' neighborhood despite its bland appearance. Exactly one week after the first kid was gunned down, another young dude was killed in almost the exact same spot as the first kid. I didn't even bother going to check out the second murder, and I didn't walk anywhere in that neighborhood by myself. The rest of the summer went like my first week there, with some gang member being killed at a rate of one every week or so.

Thankfully, Chris had a lot of friends who were as serious as I was about making it big in music. One of them was a guy known as D-Wayne. He spent most of his time shuttling between Minneapolis and Los Angeles. We went to his house to check out his setup one day. He was working on a song, but was having difficulty getting his rhymes together. I made a few suggestions not only about rhymes but about beats and loops as well. The result knocked the dude's socks off.

"Damn, Mark," D-Wayne said, "give me a week and I'll get that beat machine for you. You got major, major talent!"

D-Wayne made my day. I had no guarantee that he would keep his word but I decided to trust him. We had composed two songs together, and he was tremendously grateful for my help. He couldn't stop thanking me, which had me grinning like a Cheshire cat. So yeah, I really did trust him to keep his word.

I told Chris that I was returning to Atlanta because the gang scene was just way too intense for me. D-Wayne left for Los Angeles on the same day that I left for home. Sure enough, he called me one week later and told me to go to a local Western Union office to pick up the money for the beat machine.

CHAPTER 8

Kismet

I never knew that a man could miss a woman so much until I came home to Deirdre. I had only been in Minneapolis for a few weeks, but it felt more like a few years. Death and trouble come at young people so fast there that it ages them well beyond their years. It's not unusual to see a black man in his thirties there who already has salt-and-pepper hair, no front teeth, and a haggard face.

I purchased the beat machine on July 29, the day after I picked up the money from Western Union. I'll never forget the date because it was two days after the terrorist bombing at Centennial Olympic Park. Everyone in the city was looking over his shoulder, fearing more bombings would follow.

It took me nearly two weeks to get familiar with all of its capabilities, and another two weeks to feel comfortable operating it. Just as I was settling into my makeshift studio in our crowded apartment, I got a call from D-Wayne.

I assumed that he was calling to make sure that I received the money and had purchased the machine, but that was only one reason for his call. He was mainly calling to invite me to Los Angeles, where he had just obtained access to a state-of-the-art recording studio.

"Damn, man, I'd love to come out there, but I'm flat broke," I said.

"Don't worry about that," D-Wayne replied. "I'll send you a ticket."

I had been working with Zack White, my producer, for the better part of a year, and was reluctant to go anywhere without him. I explained my reticence to D-Wayne.

"No problem, Mark," he said. "You need to be in this studio if you wanna make it, man. I'm starting my own record label. It's called Checkmate. I want you to be my first artist. This is a golden opportunity for you, a once in a lifetime thing . . . Tell you what. I'll buy tickets for both of y'all."

After agreeing to fly out there, I hung up and started yelling with joy. I opened the first of what later proved to be many beers, blasted the radio and danced around the apartment. After the first refreshing gulp, I picked up the phone to break the good news to Deirdre, who was still at work.

That's when I caught myself. I had just told her that I wasn't going anywhere else for a while, and now I was about to back out of that promise. I thought about what I would say to her, and then dialed the number.

"Hey, Baby," I began. "I got good news and bad news."

"Tell me the bad news first," she said. "No, never mind. You're leaving town again, right?"

"Yeah, Baby" I said, "Fate's calling my name. But the good news is that I have a chance to get a record deal once I get out there. The dude who bought me the beat machine is starting his own record label."

"You sure he's legit?" she asked.

"Yeah, Sweetheart, I'm sure." I really wasn't, but it was the best opportunity I had been offered so far.

"I'm not sure how long I'll be out there. Maybe just a few weeks. If I don't land a deal, I'll come back and get that nine-to-five job that you want me to take and give up this music stuff, okay?"

"Sure, you will," Deirdre replied. "Tell me another one."

"I'm serious, Baby. I don't want to lose you. I'll do whatever I have to do for us to start a family, but I have to take this chance now or I'll never forgive myself."

"You don't have to convince me, Mark," she assured me. "I'm in your corner. Go ahead and do what you need to do."

Zack and I went to the studio in the back of The Rim Shop and started packing instruments and recording equipment. We took two guitars, the MPC beat machine, and as much other stuff as we thought we could transport.

By the time we finished, the studio was useless to anyone else. We knew that Sermon and some of the other artists were gonna be mad, but Vee had already told us to take whatever we needed to be successful in Los Angeles.

We boarded a Delta Air Lines flight for Los Angeles right after Labor Day. As we were waiting to get our luggage from the baggage carousel, we were approached by several white officers from the Los Angeles Police Department.

After what happened to Rodney King a couple of years earlier, I immediately thought that the cops were about to arrest us for some bullshit and give us an ass-whipping. I could feel my left leg shaking and my palms getting moist.

"Let me see your ticket stubs," a tall, overweight officer demanded. Zack and I quickly handed them over.

"What's the matter, Officer?" I asked humbly.

"Do you have any identification?" he asked. Zack and I showed him our driver's licenses.

"These tickets were paid for with someone else's credit card," he said. "You all better come with us."

The three officers escorted us to a small office near the baggage claim area. Once there, I was taken to one room and Zack to another. I was questioned for about thirty minutes, sweating like a pig in Florida in July. They finally took me back to the main office, where I was joined by Zack after five minutes or so.

"You're free to go," the fat cop said.

D-Wayne was rolling in dough, so I could not believe that he would have been so stupid as to use a stolen credit card to buy our tickets. Zack was convinced otherwise.

"Man, I'm about ready to go back home," he complained. "This is starting off on a really bad note. It's a bad sign. I need to cut my losses now 'cause I don't like the feel of this."

"Aw, man," I replied, "I'm sure there's a logical explanation for this. Let's give him a chance to explain what happened."

We were met by D-Wayne as we exited the terminal.

"Damn, dudes," he said looking at me, "y'all brought enough stuff with y'all, didn't y'all? No wonder it took y'all so long. We've been waitin' out here for an hour. Y'all should have mailed some of that delicate stuff."

"We damn near went to jail, that's what took us so long," Zack said disgustedly.

"No shit?" D-Wayne asked.

"No shit," Zack replied. "They thought our tickets were bought with a stolen credit card."

"Sorry about that, man," D-Wayne said smiling. "I don't use too many credit cards in my line of work. I had my sister buy the tickets on her card, but I didn't tell her who I was buying them for."

"Damn, no wonder," Zack replied. "We told them that you bought the tickets, but they kept saying that we were lying because some lady's credit card was used."

Once they ran a computer check on the woman's name, police said, she showed up at the same address as D-Wayne. Plus, she had the same last name as D-Wayne, so they released us.

We climbed into D-Wayne's black tricked-out Ford Expedition after packing it to the gills and headed for Hollywood Boulevard and Cahuenga. The state-of-the-art studio was opened in 1993 by a guy known as Kay-G. Kay-G used to fly into Atlanta a lot to make purchases at the Rim Shop and just to hang out. He was always looking for new talent in his bid to become the next big producer of hip hop.

When he first described his studio to me, it sounded like something only a white boy could afford. I had heard so many exaggerated claims about small time studios that I figured he was probably lying.

A few months after he opened it, he saw me perform at Club Oxygen. After watching me perform several times, he invited me to visit him in Los Angeles to check it out. Of course, I took him up on the offer. Since he paid for the ticket, I had nothing to lose.

Kay-G's studio was in the heart of Hollywood. In fact, it was in the same building as the studio owned by

Harris, the producer who was riding high on a hit record by Adina Howard called "A Freak Like Me." You would think that only wealthy businessmen or a major recording artist could afford the rent there.

Although Kay-G's studio was three years old, no one had ever recorded there or even used the equipment. It was in pristine condition because before anyone could use it, Kay-G was arrested, convicted, and sent off to serve several years in prison. He had left D-Wayne in charge of it.

It's impossible to describe all the different kinds of crazy people walking up and down Hollywood Boulevard every day. The song by Dionne Warwick, "Do You Know the Way to San Jose," is close to the truth. LA is full of people who came to California chasing big dreams.

Some let the dream drive them crazy and now they were homeless and out of their minds. Thousands of others were in their fifth or tenth year of waiting tables, being car hops, and Lord knows what else. Like many in the city of Lost Angels, I felt like God was guiding me and I felt that something good would happen here that would change my life forever. I was gonna make it.

Zack and I slept at D-Wayne's house the first night. The next morning, we all grabbed a bite to eat and then headed for the studio to unload the equipment. Zack and I were like kids in a candy store as we walked around the studio touching everything. The microphones, the control boards, everything had the feel of magic.

"This is it, Mark!" Zack said as we stood in the main control room. "This is our make-it-or-break-it moment."

Zack and I ate, slept, and worked around-the-clock in the studio for the next year. We ate lunch at McDonald's and dinner at Popeye's on Hollywood Boulevard near the studio almost every night. Practically the only time we left was in the morning to take a shower at the local YMCA.

We must have composed and completed as least fifty songs in that time, and we were confident that at least half of them were polished enough to record and to have hit potential.

One day we were sitting in the office listening to a song that we had just finished putting the finishing touches on when this guy I had met in Atlanta years earlier entered the studio. His name was Darius, but everybody called him D-Mack.

"What up, what up, what up!" he said as we shook hands and gave each other a hug.

"What's up, Brother?" I said. "Long time, no see. How did you know we were here?"

"I didn't," D-Mack replied. "I was leaving Livio's and something told me to stop by here. When I heard the music, I was blown away. Who is that?"

"What do you mean who is that?" I asked him, somewhat puzzled. "That's me. This is my producer, Zack White."

"Nice to meet you, Zack," he said, then resumed our conversation. "How come you never told me that you could rap? You got a lot of talent, Mark. You need to be on the radio."

"Aw, man, I appreciate that," I began. "I just assume that people know what I do. I haven't seen you in a while, so maybe that's why you didn't know. Are you living back out here now?"

"Yeah," he answered, "but I travel a lot. I have my own company now. In fact, I'm in the music business. Are you under contract yet?"

"Naw, man," I replied. "That's why we're here. We're trying to finish an album and release it on an independent label if the majors ain't interested. Who are you working for?"

"My company is called Finish Line, but I do a lot of work with Bad Boy in New York. You know Puff Daddy, right?" he asked.

"Naw . . . I mean, I met him and Suge a couple of times at Platinum House, but we don't really know each other that well."

"How much longer will you be in LA?" he asked.

"As a matter of fact, we're gonna be heading back to Atlanta in a few days," I told him. "We're wrapping things up now. Our resources have dried up. We've done what we came here to do, anyway. God is good."

Zack and I were blessed because D-Wayne had supported us for more than a year without complaining. Now, I felt like God was blessing us again by having D-Mack walk into the studio just days before we departed.

"Give me all the numbers where I can reach you, Mark, because I think we can do business. What I heard is fresh, and I'm sure Puff's gonna like it. I just started my own music production company and I'm working closely with him. Can you leave a copy of that song you were just playing with me?" he asked.

"I wish I could, man, but it's not quite ready. I have to go back home and put some finishing touches on it. Then I'll be glad to give you a copy."

"Don't take too long, man," he said as we shook hands again. "I need to let Puff hear your stuff as soon as possible. He's working with Heavy-D and some other acts right now, and they're looking for something fresh. That's a fresh sound you got, man. People gonna freak when they hear it."

"Thanks a lot, man" I said.

"Yeah, thanks," Zack chimed in.

Although I had told D-Mack that we were leaving in a few days, it wasn't true. D-Wayne wanted us to stay in Los Angeles for a few more weeks while he shopped for a record deal. After trying for more than a month, I convinced D-Wayne to stop looking and to let me go home to put a complete album package together. He agreed, but reminded us that we owed him something if we landed a deal.

"That's understood," I said.

Zack and I returned to Atlanta and started putting things together.

I had my brother and a few other artists design a front and rear cover. I drew up a marketing plan and list of prospective places to shop the album. Then we started using our contacts in local radio in an effort to get any airplay we could.

After finishing the package, I was exhausted. A week or so before Thanksgiving 1995, D-Mack called me. He was in New York visiting the Hit Factory, and he wanted me to join him so I could get a feel for what a "real" recording session looked and felt like.

"I got a surprise for you when you get here," he promised.

I boarded a United Airlines flight to New York the next morning and was in the studio with him shortly after ten o'clock. We gave each other a bear hug as record producer Tony Dofat, Heavy-D, and Herbert "McGruff" Brown looked on. I was elated to be in their presence, but I tried to conceal it. McGruff was Heavy-D's protégé. Heavy-D, in turn, was a close friend of Puff's from their teenage years in Mount Vernon.

After D-Mack made the introductions, I sat across from Dofat as he and McGruff made changes to the composition they were working on. McGruff was a highly regarded rapper from Harlem and a former member of the rap group known as Children of the Corn. The group included Mase and Cam'ron (who quit to try their hand at professional basketball), and another cat from Harlem named Lamont "Big L" Coleman.

"All right Mark," Heavy-D said as all eyes in the room focused on me, "let's see what you got."

I was flabbergasted, but once again, I tried to disguise my exuberance. Heavy-D and I went into the sound booth and started rehearsing a song called "I Don't Want to Die." Dofat finalized the cut after several takes.

I didn't suspect that the recording session with Heavy-D was a ruse, one designed to impress me with D-Mack's contacts and to make me more amenable to signing with Bad Boy Entertainment. They were buttering me up. Why, I didn't know yet.

What I did know was that Puff was on a roll. Although Biggie had been busted a couple of times recently for smoking weed, the arrests boosted record sales because it added to the image that Puff was trying to create of his artists as genuine thugs, as bad boys with street credibility.

Since stepping out of his own, Puff had already sold more than 12 million records. When Clive Davis of Arista expressed interest in a five-year contract with Bad Boy in late 1996, Puff demanded a five-million dollar advance and a credit line of $75 million. On top of that, his lawyer Kenny Meiselas convinced Arista to let Puff keep half of Bad Boy, a deal that was almost unheard of then. Puff was being compared to Berry Gordy, so Arista met almost all of his demands.

I was like a child on the day after Christmas when I returned home to Deirdre. I told every detail about the experience, and then I told her again. I'm sure that I must have gotten on her nerves, but she never let it show. That's what a good woman will do for you.

Deirdre was from Patterson, New Jersey, and her family still lived there. Since she hadn't been home since I left for Los Angeles more than a year ago, I told her to pack her bags because we were going to see her parents. With the spending money that D-Mack gave me as he saw me to La Guardia, I took Deirdre to New York to shop for some threads. I needed to present a certain image once I started hawking the album and meeting record executives, and the Big Apple has a little bit of everything in the garment district.

One of the first things dealmakers look at when you're trying to sell yourself is your image, whether it is marketable. So I bought everything I could afford that said "Curry is cash in the bank."

CHAPTER 9

Dream Merchant

Going back home was a challenge. In my long absence, Platinum House went under and the Rim Shop had long ago replaced both me and the studio equipment. Deirdre and I could scrape by on her income and on whatever odd jobs I could pick up, but I knew that I would have to find a full-time job soon if our relationship was going to last. An intelligent woman will only put up with a broke man for so long.

When I was still in Los Angeles, I met this slick dude called Tray who now lived in Atlanta. I ran into him at the Rim Shop. As we talked, I learned a lot about his background, but also about D-Mack and other cats we both knew. He told me that he knew an easy way that I could make enough money to tide me over until I finished my album. Ironically, the neighborhood where he wanted me to start selling drugs was in the same part of Atlanta where I had tried to sell crack.

I bumped into a lot of old friends from high school when I returned to the area, some of whom had major drug habits. I hadn't done hustling in a while, and consequently I had forgotten some of my old lessons. I gave an old friend named Milt some dope on credit because he was always making big money in card games. I figured he would pay me within a day or so. He kept promising to repay me for several weeks but never gave me a dime. I explained to him that I was hurting financially and that I needed my money.

I saw him leaving a local clothier one day with a load of new stuff, but he didn't see me. I felt that if he had enough money to buy all those damn clothes, then he had enough money to pay me.

I borrowed Deirdre's car and picked up my friend, Lamar. We drove over to Milt's house. I knocked on the door while Lamar stood on the porch watching the car. Milt was at his next door neighbor's house playing cards for big money. He asked me to wait until he finished his hand to speak to me, which I did. Then he asked me to wait until they finished another game.

While I waited, I asked a friend of Milt's who was watching the game to go outside and tell Lamar that it would take me a few more minutes to sort things out. The dude went to the door, then quickly turned around and walked over to me.

"Looks like you ain't goin' nowhere for a while, my man," the guy said. "The cops are all over your car."

I cracked the curtain and peeped out the window. Sure enough, police were ransacking Deirdre's car. In the trunk, I had about half a kilo of cocaine all bagged up in grams and ready to go, a scale and everything. All I could think about was how disappointed Deirdre was gonna be and how I was probably gonna be rapping in jail for the next ten years.

I called Tray and told him to contact D-Mack because I was about to be arrested on drug charges. After D-Mack posted my bond, I went over to Vee's house to tell him what happened. Bad news travels fast, as they say. Vee and Chris already knew.

"Police are probably still watching you, Mark," Vee said nervously. "It's best if you don't come around here for a while because you might get us all in trouble."

I had a court-appointed lawyer at the first hearing on the case. The lawyer was very good, as he raised the issue of illegal search-and seizure. The prosecutor must have known the case against me was in trouble because he kept requesting continuances. What seemed to be an open and shut case dragged on for months.

To research my legal options, I bought a laptop computer, got on the internet, and read as much as I could about search-and-seizure cases. I finally understood why the search of Deidre's unoccupied car was causing problems for the prosecutor, but I also realized that I might have to accept a plea bargain, as my public defender recommended.

It was difficult to concentrate on my music with the possibility of jail time hanging over me. For the first time, tensions between me and Deirdre threatened our relationship. Police wanted to seize her car as evidence, and I didn't have a car. We got a taste of what single parents who don't own a car must go through every day. It must be pure hell trying to get to and from work each day, take your kid to football practice or a music lesson or whatever else you have to do by taking public transportation.

Deirdre had to pester her friends and colleagues for transportation, and she had to endure all kinds of weather to get to work. Her patience with me was wearing thin, and I didn't blame her. I had failed her, and I was failing myself. I should have learned my lesson about selling dope the first time I got caught. That was an omen, but I became so obsessed with getting my album done that I threw common sense out of the window.

I was at one of the lowest points in my life. I lay in the bed next to Deirdre with my back facing hers, both of us pretending to be asleep, both of us afraid to touch the other. I wanted to touch her but

I was too ashamed. She didn't have to say it, but I knew that we could not last much longer unless some kind of miracle happened to one of us.

I finally drifted off to sleep. I heard a telephone ringing in my dream, or so I thought. The ringing grew more and more persistent. As I tried to figure out how to stop it, someone pushed me off a cliff. As I fell to the ground, I was amazed that I wasn't dead. The fall made me wake up.

As it turned out, the telephone really was ringing. It had awakened Deirdre, who pushed her elbow against my back and told me to wake up. She pushed me so hard that I fell out of bed, only I dreamt that it was a cliff. It was three-thirty in the morning.

"Hey, Mark," the voice on the other end said. As I cleared the cobwebs from my eyes, I realized that it was D-Mack. He was calling me from Los Angeles.

"Hey, man, what's up? Why are you calling so early?" I mumbled.

"Aw, man, I'm sorry. I forgot about the time difference," he answered. "But you won't mind me waking your ass up after I tell you who I'm sitting next to."

"Humph, I'm listening," I said.

"Puff is here with me," he said excitedly. "He liked the work that you did with Heavy-D and he likes two songs that you gave me. He wants to sign you."

I popped up in the bed, fully awake. Deirdre popped up, too, trying to listen to the conversation.

"Who is that?" she asked.

"It's D-Mack," I replied nonchalantly, covering the mouthpiece of the phone with my hand. "I think he's high or something because he's bullshittin' like Puff Daddy wants to talk to me."

"Ha!" D-Mack laughed. "You think I'm bullshitting, huh?"

A second later, another voice was on the line.

"Mark, this is Puff. I've been listening to your music, man. I want you to team up with me. I'm gonna take you places you never dreamed of. Your career is about to blow up. You interested?"

"Yes, Sir," I said. "I'm very interested."

"Okay, Mark, listen up," Puff said. "I need to meet with you today to work out some details. How soon can you get here?"

"I'm already there," I replied enthusiastically. "Seriously, let me call my producer and we'll be on the next flight out of here."

"Excellent. What's your producer's name?"

"Zack White," I replied.

"Okay, I'll tell you what," he began. "I'll have my people check on the flight and I'll leave tickets for the two of you at whatever airline that can get y'all here the fastest. My people will call you back in less than an hour. Cool?"

"Cool," I said as I grabbed Deirdre's right hand and squeezed it. Then I hung up the phone.

"Oh, my God," Deirdre said as she sat up on her knees in bed. "What did he say?"

"This is it, Baby," I replied with a smile as big as the moon. "This is it. Puff Daddy wants to sign me and he wants to do the deal in LA today. I have to grab Zack and get out of here."

"Thank you, Jesus!" Deirdre exclaimed. "My baby's gonna be a star!"

"Amen," I chimed in. "Thank the Lord!"

Zack and I met Puff and D-Mack that evening at a five-star restaurant on Sunset Boulevard. I had seen him any number of times at Platinum House, but this was the first time that we were speaking man to man. While I was never impressed with his wealth or his persona, you had to respect a young black man who had made so much money so fast. But the topic of conversation was about to knock my socks off.

"Mark, welcome to LA," Puff began and he sat down. A waiter rushed to the table at breakneck speed. Since Puff was paying for it, I ordered a huge meal, but I only had one drink since I had to keep a clear head.

"Mark," he said as he leaned back in his chair," all of my artists have big homes and nice cars, a pocket full of cash and money in the bank. I treat my artists the way I would want to be treated, with dignity and respect. Know what I'm sayin'?"

"I hear 'ya," I said somewhat flatly, not wanting him to think that

I was an easy mark, so to speak.

"I'm out here on a multimillion-dollar deal right now, and you can be a part of it," he continued. "I'm working on the soundtrack for the new version of "Godzilla" that's coming out in a year or so. Problem is, Mark, I want the song to be the freshest shit anybody's ever heard. D-Mack played some of your stuff for me and I really liked it. But right now, I want you to take this track that I've been working on and see what you can do with it."

At that moment, I was unable to hide my joy. All I could think of was that the first song I write for Bad Boy is gonna be featured in a big budget movie and on a soundtrack!

"No problem, Puff," I said smiling. "I'll get right on it. You gonna have a hit on your hands, that's for damn sure."

Everybody laughed. "That's what I'm talkin' 'bout," Puff said. "That's what I'm talkin' 'bout. I need that hit, player. Put some balls on that bitch for me."

Zack and I headed back to the suite. We could order anything we wanted on Puff's tab, so we began with a bottle of champagne. At first I did more drinking than thinking, but I promised myself to make up for it the next day.

It seemed like such an easy assignment when I agreed to it. But as I listened to Puff's song, I couldn't think of any words or rhymes that would give the song pizzazz and hit potential. The music was from Led Zeppelin's 1975 hit, "Kashmir." Jimmy Page was going to lay down some fresh guitar licks for the soundtrack with Puff rapping to the music. Puff had been trying to write lyrics for the song for months and had gotten nowhere. Facing a deadline, he wanted me to finish the song in no time flat.

After several days without progress, I called Puff to tell him that I was drawing a blank. I was trying to write lyrics that would sound like Puff had written them, so I kept on tearing up the paper and starting over.

"Don't worry, Mark," he said. "Keep trying."

Every time I came back with a verse he would say the same thing. "That's not it, player."

After a few more days and more rejections, I called him again and told him that I just couldn't think of any more verses that would make sense in the context of the movie scene where the song was supposed to fit it.

"So you ain't up to it?" he said somewhat impatiently.

"Naw, man," I began, "it's not that. I could write something. I'm just not sure it will represent you."

"Tell you what, Mark," he said sternly. "I got somebody else who can do this if you can't handle it, all right?"

I could see my recording career jumping off the hotel balcony with those words. If the song was trashed by the critics, it could mean the end of my career not only at Bad Boy but at any other studio as well. When Puff said that he would hand the assignment off to someone else, something deep in my soul began stirring.

"Give me a little more time, Puff," I pleaded. "I'll give you a hit."

"That's what I'm talkin' 'bout, player. You gotta believe in yourself, baby."

Believing in myself wasn't the problem. My father had schooled me well on the importance of believing in myself, on the importance of not placing someone on a pedestal because they had more money or better looks or a better education than you. "Rich people go broke every day, good looks fade every day, and the world is full of educated fools," he'd say. "So the bottom line is that we're all equal even when it doesn't look that way on the surface."

That night at dinner, Puff apologized for being curt with me earlier. "The problem is that you don't feel me right now," he said. "I have no problem with that because you don't really know me. I'll tell – "

"No," I interjected. "It's not that I don't –"

He interrupted me and said: "Let me finish. Come and join me on my tour. You'll get to know me a lot better and it'll be a good experience for you. You'll be prepared to do your own live shows once your album comes out if you learn the basics now."

"You serious?" I asked like a kid who's just been offered a free trip to Disneyland.

"I never joke around, Mark," he said. "We could work on the song together on the jet and on the road. We still have a little time before it's due."

CHAPTER 10

Biggie and Tupac

I took my first ride on a private jet the next morning with Puff and his entourage. We flew to Chicago for a concert, and then to New York, and finally back to Los Angeles. Unfortunately, the "No Way Out" tour wasn't limited to a solid block of time. We would have two engagements one week and three more two weeks later. This pattern went on for several months. The tour included thirty cities in all to promote Puff's debut album.

I spent so much time learning Puff's songs, dance routines, and getting used to flying at a moment's notice that I hardly had time to work on the song for the soundtrack as the deadline closed in on me.

Once I learned more about Puff, I realized why he was too preoccupied to work on the song. He had been in a funk for months before I arrived in Los Angeles. He was expecting a child by his girlfriend, Kim Porter, but he hadn't spent much time with her due to the tour. The main reason for his dark mood, however, was the murder in March 1997 of Christopher Wallace, the most lucrative artist in the Bad Boy family.

Wallace, better known as Notorious B.I.G. and Biggie Smalls (borrowed from a character in a blaxploitation era movie, but Smalls is also the maiden name of Puff's mother, Janice), was Bad Boy's first superstar, the artist who made Puff a millionaire. A former honor student-turned-drug dealer in Brooklyn, Biggie gave Puff and Bad Boy Entertainment legitimacy and street credibility. He remains one of the most imitated rappers in the world.

Despite his amazing record sales, however, Biggie was not faring much better than his Jamaican-born parents. Like a lot of artists, his contract was worded in such a way that he received little money after a laundry list of "expenses" was deducted. In fact, Biggie resorted to selling dope and homemade duplicates of his CDs from the trunk of his car just to earn spending money. That fact was little known outside of New York.

Biggie's mother, Voletta Wallace, tried to tell him that Puff was a shyster, but Biggie didn't want to hear it. It's hard to convince a poor man that the person who put $25,000 in his pocket and promises to make him rich is hustling him. By the time Biggie realized that Puff was burning him – he signed a long-term contract in 1993 that enslaved him to Puff – it was too late.

Once Biggie realized that he had been duped not only with the Uptown contract but the Bad Boy deal as well, he started to resent Puff for taking advantage of him. He compared Puff to the con men with whom he had dealt with during his drug-dealing days.

"I'm signed for a while," he said in 1994, "so I'm gonna handle my business. But I really can't see myself doing this shit too much longer because it's too foul for me. If I want to deal with some foul niggas, I'd rather be on the street level, not no business shit 'cause they could get over on me."

In early 1997, Biggie was crowning the hip hop charts nationally and internationally. Whenever there was an awards show or major hip hop event that Puff wanted to attend, he insisted on dragging Biggie along. That was the case on March 9, when Soul Train held its annual music awards show in Los Angeles.

According to Puff biographer Ronin Ro, Puff claimed that Biggie wanted to stay in LA for a bit longer and begged him to attend an after party, and also claimed that he made the call to Voletta Wallace after Biggie got shot. As usual, Puff paints himself in heroic strokes. Puff's version, like his account of his activities during an earlier tragedy, was riddled with lies.

Biggie didn't want to attend the *Vibe* party for a number of reasons. His wife, Faith Evans, was pregnant and they were having marital problems. He was stressed out about his new album. His right leg, injured in a car accident on the New Jersey turnpike, was giving him a lot of pain. Then there was the matter of the occasional anonymous threats against his life in the aftermath of Tupac's death.

Puff, Biggie, and other Bad Boy artists had been hunkered down at a hotel in Los Angeles for nearly a month before the Soul Train awards show. Although they had initially expected trouble from Bloods upon their arrival, things were relatively quiet. Some people think that nothing happened because Suge was still in jail and because Puff kept a low profile.

Biggie and Junior M.A.F.I.A. had worked so hard on Puff's new album that they were exhausted and bored by the time of the show. In fact, Biggie told Puff that he was leaving LA the day after the Soul Train awards to rest and let his leg heal properly.

The first sign of friction began at the Soul Train awards. When Biggie went on stage to accept an award, he was loudly booed by a large group of West Coast rappers. The negative feedback from the audience reinforced Biggie's determination to leave Los Angeles the next afternoon. He told Puff that he would go to the studio to finish his verses on the "Victory" track, and then he was going home.

After completing "Victory," he spent the rest of the session putting the finishing touches on his new album with the ominous title of "Life After Death," Biggie returned to his hotel room and started packing. That's when the trouble started.

It wasn't Biggie calling Puff, but rather Puff pleading with Biggie to stay in Los Angeles for one more night. According to knowledgeable friends at Bad Boy and members of Junior M.A.F.I.A., Puff called Biggie at least a dozen times. Biggie was adamant that he didn't want to stick around, but Puff wouldn't take no for an answer. Despite what his instincts were telling him, Biggie caved in to Puff's demands.

Six months before the Soul Train awards, Tupac was in Las Vegas with Suge Knight to attend the Mike Tyson - Bruce Seldon heavyweight boxing match at the MGM Grand on September 7. As Suge, Tupac, and their entourage were walking through the hotel lobby, they spotted Orlando "Baby Lane" Anderson, a well-known member of the Crips gang who was suspected of leading gang members in the brutal beating of a Death Row employee outside a shoe store a month before the Tyson bout.

Tupac repeatedly punched Anderson who, as he fell to the floor, was pummelled by members of the entourage. Hotel security cameras also recorded Suge kicking him.

Word of the beating travelled among Crips in the vicinity of the hotel and in Crips territory in Las Vegas. Tupac, Suge, their entourage, and a phalange of Bloods hopped in their cars and the caravan headed for Club 662 (also known as Club "MOB" because those letters correspond to those numbers on the telephone pad, and MOB is an acronym for Member of Bloods).

Tupac was in the front passenger seat as Suge drove his Beamer (BMW) past the Maxim Hotel. When they reached a stop light, a white Cadillac pulled along beside them and a man in the back seat fired thirteen shots at Tupac. He was struck once in the left arm and thigh, and two bullets hit him in the chest. By the time police rushed him to University Medical Center, Tupac was in grave condition. He died six days later.

Since none of the thirteen bullets hit Suge, people speculated that he might have had some involvement. They pointed at that Tupac had publicly revealed his plans to leave Death Row because he suspected that Suge was ripping him off. Suge claimed that one of the bullets lodged in his head, but that turned out to be a total fabrication.

Another rumor had it that Biggie had bought one of the guns used in the hit, and that Biggie had put a million-dollar bounty for Tupac's life. Biggie gave numerous interviews in which he denied any involvement in Tupac's death. His mother, Puff, and his friends all told reporters that Biggie was in a New York studio on the night that Tupac was killed, and they produced copies of studio records to prove it. But despite his protestations of innocence, conspiracy theories abounded about Biggie's alleged role in Tupac's death.

It was a sad ending to what was once a cool friendship. A few years earlier, when Biggie was down on his luck but Tupac was riding high as a rapper and movie star, the two men shared a tiny apartment in Harlem. Tupac let the 6-foot, 300-pound aspiring rapper sleep on a sofa there while he tried to launch his career. Two years later, Biggie was a major recording star and it was Tupac who needed a helping hand.

In September 1996, as threats between East Coast and West Coast rappers intensified – it was really a war of words between the Bloods and the Crips – Minister Conrad Muhammad of Nation of Islam's Harlem mosque called for a peace summit. Suge, Puff and Big-gie did not attend.

Suge and Puff were also once good friends, but egos, misunderstandings and false friends turned them into bitter enemies. By the time of the summit, Biggie had grown weary of Puff, as had a number of other Bad Boy artists. The rotund rapper had recently launched his own record label, and in fact had signed and recorded its first artist, Junior M.A.F.I.A.. Just as Tupac was planning to leave Death Row at the time of his death, Biggie was about to break away from Bad Boy.

When Biggie agreed to go to the *Vibe* party with Puff, maybe he thought that it would be the last time that Puff forced him to do something against his will. Maybe this would be his parting gift to the mentor that he was ready to abandon to become a mentor himself. Just as

Puff had once bet his dreams on Biggie, Biggie had bet his dreams on making Junior M.A.F.I.A. recording stars.

The Soul Train after party was held at the Peterson Automotive Museum on the very busy Wilshire Boulevard. Sponsored by *Vibe* magazine and Qwest Records (both owned by Quincy Jones), the party was supposed to be a hush-hush affair for VIPs only. The problem with that is that once a VIP-poseur gets invited to an exclusive party, he blabbers about it and before long everybody in town knows about it.

When Biggie and Puff arrived at the museum in separate cars, what Biggie saw left him feeling betrayed by Puff. True enough, he saw Quincy Jones, Russell Simmons, Queen Latifah and dozens of other celebrities inside. But the party was hardly private. More than 2,000 uninvited guests were there. The scene outside the club museum was total chaos, and there was no way for his security team and the limited LAPD officers to handle the crowd.

To placate the huddled masses and to avoid trouble, security let as many fans in as possible. But in doing so, the museum became overcrowded and someone called police. Within minutes, police and firefighters arrived and demanded that everyone vacate the building.

Puff rode in the car ahead of Biggie.

Excessive artificial lighting on Wilshire reminds a visitor of the strip in Las Vegas or Times Square, where the sun never sets. Anyone committing of crime near the museum would most likely be easy to identify due to all the bright lights, so there no was reason for Biggie to feel vulnerable.

While Biggie's car was waiting at the stoplight, another car pulled up and sprayed him with gunfire. Sure enough, several witnesses said that they got a good look at the shooter, and someone caught part of the shooting on tape.

The hit was nearly a carbon copy of the murder of Tupac. When the gunfire ended and the shooters sped away, Puff and the others got out of their vehicles and rushed to Biggie's car.

"Oh, God, please let him pull through," Puff cried as Biggie struggled to breathe. When Puff tried to close the car door, he couldn't because Biggie had fallen backward and his leg was in the way of the car door. Damien Butler, (Biggie's friend since childhood), and a couple of other dudes helped Puff lift Biggie's leg upward and push him into the car enough to close the door.

Some people have tried to argue that Biggie might have survived if he had been taken to a hospital that was only two blocks away from the museum instead of Cedars-Sinai Medical Center, which was two miles from the museum. Most people know better. The doctors said that Biggie was probably dead the minute the gunfire stopped. He had been shot at least seven times in the chest and stomach by a killer using a .9mm gun.

Puff also told Ronin Ro that members of Junior M.A.F.I.A. were too grief-stricken to call Biggie's mother to give her the bad news, so he called her. Once again, that was a lie. Voletta Wallace and other witnesses agree that Puff was a basket case that night.

"Puff was freakin' out," Li'l Cease said in a recent documentary. Cease said that while he and members of Junior M.A.F.I.A. were trying to figure out how to get Biggie back home, Puff went back to his hotel, grabbed his stuff, and was on a plane for New York in less than three hours.

Ms. Wallace initially refused to believe Damien. She put her sister-in-law on the phone, and Damien yelled through tears that Biggie was dead. Even then, Ms. Wallace refused to believe it. It was only after she called Faith Evans, Biggie's wife, that reality began to take hold.

Damien, Cease, and the others promised Ms. Wallace that they would remain with Biggie until she arrived at the hospital. When they told her that Puff had already flown back to New York, it only confirmed for her what she had been trying to tell her only child for years, that Puff's allegiance was to the almighty dollar, not to him or anyone else.

In an interview the day after Biggie's funeral, Puff claimed that he and Biggie had been fighting to let people know from the very beginning that "we were never with that whole East Coast-West Coast thing, we were not about that," but police and insiders knew better.

Puff demanded that his artist talk like thugs, walk like thugs, dress like thugs and behave like thugs. When he was asked to explain the type of artists he wanted on his label, he said that he wanted artists with attitudes . . . like they're mad even when they're singing."

Although he had grown up on the right side of the tracks, Puff wanted everyone to believe just the opposite. He surrounded himself with social misfits, and he began letting more and more gangsters creep into Bad Boy not only as artists but as managers, bodyguards and rank-and-file employees.

This false bravado may have cost Biggie his life, and gave Puff his first reality check in a long time. "You can have all the success and money in the world, but at the end of the day it really doesn't mean a thing. I can't be happy right now because my best friend is dead. I know God doesn't give you anything you can't handle, but I'm really struggling with it, man. I'm having a tough time here."

Within days of the funeral, Puff called Faith Evans and other former and current Bad Boy artists into the studio to cut a single paying homage to Biggie. Using the music from the Police's hit, "Every Breath You Take," Faith sang lead vocals on "I'll Be Missing You," which was an instant runaway hit following its release in late May 1997.

Puff called Biggie the "founding father of my dream," the day the song was released. He said that the proceeds from the song would go to a trust fund for Wallace's three-year-old daughter Tyanna and his seven-month-old son, Christopher. "I'm going to make sure that I take care of his family for the rest of my life. His family is my family."

It was typical public relations for Puff, who never showed humility unless his "dream" was in jeopardy or unless he was facing public outrage. He had exploited Biggie in life and now he was exploiting his death. Biggie's murder was the second time that Puff's ego and way of doing business had resulted in calamity. The first incident happened at the beginning of his career.

In late 1991, Puff promoted a "celebrity" basketball game in Harlem between a team he led and a team captained headed by his friend Heavy-D. The game was held in the gymnasium at the City University of New York (CUNY). Although the auditorium had a maximum capacity of 2,730, Puff had sold more than 5,000 tickets before game day, December 28.

In addition to the ticket holders, hundreds of kids hoping to buy tickets at the door showed up. By game time an estimated 5,500 kids were determined to get into that gym. Predictably, a shoving match started as soon as the doors opened and most of the kids who fell got trampled. When police finally restored order, there were nine dead teen-agers at the bottom of the pile and dozens more required medical attention.

An official investigation proved that Puff had lied to CUNY officials about obtaining insurance to cover any accidents at the event, that he lied about overselling tickets to the game, that he lied about having adequate security, and that he lied about remaining with the victims until medical assistance arrived.

Although Puff told police and the media that he was more concerned about the victims than profits from the game, witnesses testified that they saw him and a white woman walking away from the ticket table around seven o'clock, and that Puff was holding big bulging white money bags. Puff Daddy Productions earned about $25,000 from the event, but it had to be turned over to the deputy mayor of New York until the probe into the disaster was finished.

Andre Harrell, Puff's mentor at Uptown Records, hired the famous lawyer William Kunstler to defend his reckless employee, and then placed Puff on an "indefinite suspension." Kunstler tried to cast blame on the university, but the parents of the dead children weren't buying that. Once the investigation was over, Harrell quietly fired Puff, telling insiders that he was "too arrogant" for his own good.

Families of the victims filed wrongful death actions against Puff, but Puff's lawyers fought them tooth and nail. Some lawsuits were tied up in litigation for years, and for a decade in a couple of cases.

Puff had been able to put the nightmare of the children's deaths behind him until Biggie died. The media noted that trouble seemed to follow the young multimillionaire. News stories reminded people of Puff's role in the CUNY deaths.

CHAPTER 11

Thug Life

It was only a matter of time before Puff's pretending to be a real thug would catch up with him. Melvin Combs, Puff's daddy, was a true thug, a heroin dealer who sold the soothing poison to the people of Harlem and the Bronx. At the end of the day, though, Melvin slept in the suburbs where he did everything possible to keep his son away from people like himself and his victims.

New York's finest were unable to make serious criminal charges stick against Melvin, probably because so many of them were on the take. Melvin sold so much dope that he usually had tens of thousands of dollars hidden in the cab that he drove as a front.

In the early 1970s, tons of heroin from Southeast Asia poured into New York City from Marseilles, an event immortalized in the movie, "The French Connection." Because the drug conspiracy was international, the FBI joined a select group of New York detectives to penetrate the ring.

Informants eventually fingered Melvin Combs as a major player. Investigators wondered how a man who drove a cab could pay cash for a Cadillac, a fancy home, and buy custom-tailored clothes and furs for himself and his wife. After placing him under surveillance, investigators linked Combs to a dozen people who ran a syndicate that distributed more that $5 million worth of heroin a year in Harlem, the Bronx, and Westchester County.

Based on leads from informants, Combs was placed under surveillance in early 1971. In November, after watching Combs make a transaction, police arrested him. He had $45,000 in his pocket and pounds of heroin in his car. A few weeks after his arrest, police raided the home of one of Melvin's associates, and then raided the heroin mill where Combs got his supply. As a result of the bust, Combs must have guessed that his days were numbered. The syndicate knew that the feds had flipped someone, and Combs was as likely a suspect as any.

On January 26 – a mere two months after his arrest – police found Melvin Combs in Central Park slumped over the steering wheel of his cab. He had been shot in the head at close range.

Puff's daddy was 33 years old when he died. Sean John Combs was two and Keisha, the daughter born within days of Melvin's arrest, was two months old. In explaining to Puff why his father would not be coming home again, Janice Combs told him that Melvin had been killed in an "automobile accident."

Puff and Keisha believed their mother's story about the death of their father until Puff started attending the private, predominantly white Mount Saint Michael High School in Mount Vernon, New York.

In the course of a class assignment, he ventured into the microfilm archives of the *New York Times* to seek stories about his father. He ultimately found a story dated February 24, 1973 with the headline: "Ten

Found Guilty of Heroin Charge; Convicted of Taking Part in $5-Million-A-Year Plot."

Sometime after the discovery, Puff became more rebellious. He developed an interest in a new genre of music called hip hop. Before long, he was sneaking out of the house at night to hang around clubs that catered to young blacks. He was usually accompanied by a small group of friends who formed a gang known as the "Valley Mob." One was Anthony "Wolf" Jones and the other was Lamont "Riz" Girdy.

They chose "Valley Mob" because they spent a lot of time hanging out in the Bronx in an area called "the Valley." It was a perfect fit for Puff, who seemed to want to be a "bad boy" by night like his mob-linked father and the fashionable mama's boy by day.

Since everyone around him had tough-sounding nicknames, Sean Combs decided to adopt one himself. He chose "Puff Daddy." The name evoked images of someone who was probably a marijuana kingpin or someone who could smoke more dope than anyone else, which was exactly the kind of image he wanted.

Wolf and Girdy both graduated from the Bronx's Harry Truman High School in 1983, where they were popular among their classmates. While Girdy tried to keep focused on a career in music, Wolf took the whole mob thing seriously. As a result, when Girdy moved to Atlanta to pursue his dreams, Wolf was racking up a criminal record and ended up getting convicted of attempted murder in 1991.

When Wolf was released a couple of years later, Puff gave him a job as a bodyguard. By 1994, Girdy's musical dreams had soured and he joined Wolf. Another friend, Jason Brown, was also added.

After attending Howard University for two years, Puff dropped out to pursue a career as a music promoter and producer. He worked for Uptown Records until the trampling incident.

At the time, there were really only two major hip hop labels, Def Jam and Ruthless Records. Shortly after Suge Knight, a former bodyguard to several entertainers formed Death Row Records in 1992, Puff created Bad Boy Entertainment.

As their names suggest, hip hop labels attracted young black men with links to gangs or who had serious felony convictions, or both.

Among them were three Haitians: Jacques "Haitian Jack" Agnant, James "Jimmy Henchmen" Rosemond, and Walter "King Tut" Johnson. All three men had extensive criminal records, and all three were trying to forge their way into the music business.

Rosemond had a reputation as a ruthless thug. A long keloid scar running from his left ear to his chin was a testament to his once violent lifestyle. Henchmen served two years on Rikers Island for a few of his crimes. "I was there running my shit," he recalled in a recent interview, when a "little knucklehead dude" called Curtis "50 Cent" Jackson came to Rikers.

After his release, Henchmen started his own record label which he called "Henchman Entertainment." He had an artist known as Li'l Shawn whom he was trying to develop, but he felt that he needed a big name rapper in order to launch Shawn's first record.

At some point before August 1994, a beef developed between Tut and Tupac Shakur. The two hadn't seen each other for a while until, Tupac recounted, he bumped into Tut and Biggie on the street. Knowing of Tut's reputation for shooting first and taking names later, Tupac began to reach for his gun when Biggie told him to chill. Tupac granted Biggie's request, but the exchanged damaged their friendship since Biggie was a friend of his enemy.

Most people feared Tut. Tut had a criminal record going back to 1979, when he went on robbery and burglary rampages in Brooklyn. He was 19 years old. After finishing a brief prison term, Tut was released. In June 1982 he robbed 300 Jehovah's Witnesses at the Kingdom Hall (church) attended by his own mother. He was sentenced from two to six years. While he was out on bail, Tut and his crew robbed a city bus full of passengers. He got the same sentence, but they ran concurrently, and he was free in 1984 after serving less than two years.

In 1988, he was sentenced to eight years imprisonment on weapons and robbery charges, but was released in October 1991 after only serving three years. In January 1993, Tut and six cohorts robbed a store in Manhattan and Eddie's Unisex Barber Shop in Brooklyn and then hailed a gypsy cab to escape. An undercover policeman ended up a para-

Thug Life

plegic as a result of the shootout during the escape in which Tut used his eight-year-old son as a shield. Incredibly, Tut was acquitted.

In February 1994, he was sent back to prison for robbery and violating parole. Instead of finishing the eight-year sentence, Tut served six months. After being freed in August, he showed up on Puff's doorstep.

Tut's crew earned money mainly through robbery, burglary, and extortion. According to informants, Tut ran the gang with military precision. His gang had a reputation for robbing drug dealers and stash houses.

Puff knew this when Tut showed up at Bad Boy and asked to meet with him. If Puff was really a thug, he wouldn't have given Tut the time of day. He would have known that Tut was trying to mole his way to the control room of Bad Boy Entertainment.

"I can be beneficial to you," Tut said. "You don't have to give me anything, no salary or nothing. I have income coming in. I just need someone to educate me about the music business."

"Man," Puff replied, "I heard some real bad things about you. I ain't looking for more problems."

Tut kept pleading his case and Puff kept resisting. It wasn't until Tut lost his temper and told Puff not to judge him by what other people have said that Puff caved in.

"I'll give you a chance," Puff said. "The first thing you need to do is read *All You Need to Know about the Music Business.* Learn it by heart."

Even after Tut started working with Puff, he continued to lead a thug's life. Not only did Puff know about how Tut earned money, but he reportedly paid some of his legal bills.

Although Tupac was in New York shooting a movie in 1994, he had spent the advance money and was broke. Two seemingly unrelated events would end up nearly costing him his life. Tupac befriended Agnant while shooting "Above the Rim," in which he was playing the part of a thug named Birdie.

People cautioned him about Agnant's reputation as a gangster, but Agnant won him over by spending more than $5,000 on him within a few days of meeting him. Tupac was so impressed that he decided to model Birdie after him. It wasn't long, however, before Agnant's outlaw ways got Tupac into trouble.

Agnant took Tupac to a dance hall where he introduced him to a woman who seemed to be a fan. A subsequent hotel encounter with the woman led to rape charges against Tupac, Agnant, and two others. Although the encounter between Tupac and the woman was consensual, he ended up being charged with rape, a felony. Agnant, who engaged in nonconsensual acts with the woman, was only charged with misdemeanors. Tupac smelled a frame-up.

Tupac didn't heed the warnings about Agnant until after the bizarre rape case. After he was released on bail, Tupac was having lunch with fellow actor Mickey Rourke and a reporter for the *New York Daily News.* The reporter asked Tupac about rumors that he was set up. In response, Tupac called Agnant a "snitch" and a paid government informant. The reporter printed Tupac's statements in his column the next day.

During this same time frame, Rosemond called Tupac and offered him $7,000 to make a cameo on an album being recorded by a new artist known as Li'l Shawn. Since he was broke, Tupac reluctantly agreed. He was told to come to Quad Recording Studios on the night of November 30. Upon his arrival, he rang the bell.

Rosemond stuck his head out of a window and told Tupac and his two associates to enter the building and come to a studio upstairs. In the studio with Rosemond at the time were Biggie Smalls and Junior M.A.F.I.A. members, Puff, Andre Harrell of Uptown Records, and perhaps ten others.

As Tupac entered the building, he was shot several times by two men wearing caps and army fatigues. After being left for dead, Tupac managed to make it upstairs to try to get help. Although he considered himself friendly with Puff and Biggie, Tupac was startled when neither of them nor anyone else in the building offered him assistance.

Suddenly, three policemen showed up (the same three, it turned out, who had arrested him and testified against him in the rape case). Tupac also discovered after the attack that Johnson was one of several Haitian gangsters affiliated with Puff and Bad Boy.

A few weeks after Tupac was shot, and in one of the worst public relations blunders in history, Bad Boy released Biggie's song, "Who Shot 'Ya." Although it didn't mention Tupac by name (the song was actually recorded in September, a full two months before the shooting), everyone believed he was the subject of the lyrical taunt.

Tupac was furious. So was Suge Knight, who was trying to get Tupac to sign with Death Row. Together, they plotted their revenge. Tupac allegedly became friendly with Faith Evans, who was married to Biggie at the time. He and Suge later gave an interview in which Tupac claimed that he had seduced Faith and Suge claimed that he had an affair with Mysa Hilton, Puff's former girlfriend and mother of his first child.

Tupac cut a song called "Hit 'Em Up," in which he called Biggie numerous names and reiterated his claims about Faith. He also said that she had purchased clothing for him – in other words, that he had pimped her.

After Tupac got killed and Tut was rumored to be a suspect, Puff got amnesia when investigators asked about the night of the studio shooting and his relationship with Tut. Despite growing evidence that he knew Tut, Puff kept denying it.

"Walter Johnson?" Puff said when reporters asked him about Tut a few weeks after Tupac was killed. "I don't know any Walter Johnson."

Tut later became the first New Yorker to be prosecuted under the federal "three strikes" law. In the slammer, Tut allegedly started telling people why he shot Tupac.

"Tupac is a sucker," Tut told an informant. "He's not a real gangster. He needed to be disciplined, so I shot him."

Tut wasn't in the studio at Quad the night that Tupac was shot, so his claim has credibility. At the time, Agnant was working for Harrell, which explained his presence.

Since landing the rapper known as "The Game" as one of his artists, Rosemond has claimed that he had nothing to do with the shooting. He castigated Tupac for implicating him on a song he recorded after the shooting. While protesting his innocence, Rosemond made several interesting comments in an interview with *Vibe* magazine. He said that a few weeks after the shooting, he ran into Tupac at a D'Angelo concert.

"The whole Death Row clique was up in there," he said, "and I remember going to him – I had some Crip dudes with me – and I said: Dude, you gotta stop telling people that shit [about his alleged involvement in the shooting]."

As Tupac listened, Rosemond said: "Why you blaming Puffy and Biggie? Them niggas ain't got nothin' to do with this [the shooting]. . . Nobody came to rob you. They came to discipline you, and that's what happened."

The problem with Rosemond's argument is this: how would he know that the shooters had not come to rob Tupac? How would he know that their purpose was – as King Tut told a jailhouse informant – merely to discipline Tupac? And third, what did Tupac need disciplining for? As Arsenio Hall used to say, it's one of those things that make you go "hmmm . . ."

By the time Tupac got killed in September 1996, police had a snitch so close to Biggie that they knew every time he lit up a joint, touched a pistol, or thought about doing something illegal.

For instance, a snitch told police that if they acted fast they could find Biggie sitting in his car smoking dope with Li'l Cease and other members of Junior M.A.F.I.A.. That was in August 1996. Then, two days after Tupac was killed, a rat told police that they could find Biggie and Junior M.A.F.I.A. members smoking dope at Biggie's house. Sure enough, police arrested them and seized two guns with laser-targeting devices and a box a hollow-point bullets.

CHAPTER 12

A Monster Hit

As Puff dealt with his demons, a phone call from Deirdre reminded me that I needed to return to Atlanta to deal with mine, namely the cocaine charges stemming from the search of her car.

I had read up on the law and educated myself about the possible repercussions. I mentioned to Puff on several occasions that I had to hire a lawyer or else I'd be leaving the "No Way Out" tour for a "No Way Out of Jail" tour.

"Don't worry about it, Mark," Puff said as we sat by the pool at the Beverly Hills Hotel. "I'll have you talk to Johnnie when we get to Atlanta. I got you covered."

A few weeks later, Puff and I were sharing a table in the VIP lounge at an upscale restaurant on Peachtree with none other than Johnnie Cochran. After quick introductions and some chitchat, Puff turned to me and said: "Tell Johnnie about the problem you got goin' on here."

I told Cochran about the search of Deirdre's car. I also told him that I had not hired a lawyer, and that I definitely couldn't afford him right now. He smiled and replied, "No, but Puff can. Is he got your back?" The three of us laughed, first at Cochran's use of street slang, and secondly because he wanted to make sure that Puff intended to pay him up front.

Thinking that Cochran's next words would be "Sure, Mark, I can represent you," I started smiling like a man who'd just won the lottery. I couldn't believe that the same lawyer who helped O.J. Simpson walk was going to represent me. An acquittal, I figured, is all but assured.

"Let me give you some advice, Mark," Cochran said as he leaned toward me. "You should hire the best criminal attorney in Atlanta because he'll be familiar with the judges here and will therefore be in a better position to cut a deal for you."

Hell, I already knew that. "If I could have afforded the best local attorney or any damn attorney," I thought to myself as I looked contemptuously at him, "I wouldn't be here smiling in your face, sucka."

The next day, I began asking around about the best local defense attorneys. The consensus was that I couldn't go wrong with Bruce Harvey, who represented one of the suspects in Atlanta's infamous murder-for-hire case against Fredric Tokars. Harvey, I was told, had helped a lot of scoundrels beat drug possession charges.

As part of our defense, I got a letter from Puff on official Bad Boy letterhead stating that I was essential to the successful completion of the "No Way Out" tour. My attorney sent the original to the judge trying my case and placed a copy in my case file which he kept in his office. After several meetings with the prosecutor, Harvey worked out a plea agreement.

When the judge asked me what my plea was, I stood before him in a brand new pen-striped suit and said: "Guilty, Your Honor."

I felt dizzy and my legs felt wobbly as he looked at me and started reciting the facts in my case the way judges do just before they announce your sentence. As I tried to take a deep breath, the judge said: "I hereby sentence you to 140 . . . hours of community service."

Damn! I couldn't believe my ears. For a minute I almost passed out because I thought he was gonna say 140 years in prison.

"Thank you, Your Honor," I smiled. "Thank you, thank you, thank you."

I turned to Harvey's assistant (a female attorney who actually did most of the negotiating), shook her hand, and began thanking her profusely as well. I turned to assess the prosecutor's reaction, but he was looking down at his notes and readying for the next case. I gave Deirdre a long tight squeeze.

We walked as fast as we could out of that courthouse before the judge changed his mind or something. After a night of celebrating with my sweetheart, I boarded a flight back to Los Angeles.

When Puff told me that he had me covered, I assumed that he meant that he would cover my legal expenses. Harvey did not come cheap. Once I received his bill, I showed it to Puff, thinking that he would pay it. At the time that he told me that he had the fees covered, he was still waiting on me to finish the song for the "Godzilla" soundtrack. Now that the first draft was finished, he was saying something different.

"I gotta send this to the accountants first, all right? I'll let them handle it. Stay focused on finishing the song and the tour. This shit ain't no problem."

But apparently it was. Deirdre called me month after month, saying that Harvey's office had sent a number of reminders saying that it had yet to receive any payments on the huge legal bill. I was starting to feel bad because I knew that I would be prison if Harvey's team weren't such good lawyers.

After nearly a year passed without Puff paying as much as a nickel on my bill, I called Harvey and promised to pay him as soon as I signed a record deal in a few months. He was happy to hear from me, wished me well, and said that he looked forward both to my success and to stamping "paid in full" on my account.

I had relied on Puff's promises, and now I had to deal with the fact that his word could not be relied upon and that my trust and faith in him had been misplaced. While Puff was paying for my meals during the tour, I was not getting a salary, so money for basic living expenses was hard to come by.

Puff called himself doing us a favor by letting us sell some of the batch of front-row ticket seats that he purchased from Ticketmaster at a huge discount and then sold at the arena's entrance for a measly five dollars above face value. Whoever sold the ticket got to keep the five-dollar profit. The problem was people were afraid to buy the tickets because the price was too low to be believable; people thought they were counterfeit. Consequently, I rarely sold more than two or three. Whatever tickets remained unsold were returned to Ticketmaster for a refund.

Out of frustration, at the next engagement I asked Puff to give me and Zack five backstage passes each instead of the front row tickets. I ran to the entrance of the arena and started hawking the passes for $500 apiece. I sold all five in less than twenty minutes. Zack did, too. We were able to do that for the next two concerts, but security started complaining about all the strangers backstage and in the dressing room area. Puff pulled the plug, sending us back to nickel-and-diming.

"Damn, Zack," I replied, "I'm sorry that things have worked out this way, but I couldn't just say no. You know that. This is a once in a lifetime opportunity. You think I don't miss my lady? You think that I like all this damn traveling? I mean, it was fun at first but this shit gets old fast. I'm already worn out."

Zack looked at me and smiled because my exhaustion must have been obvious. I was stealing shuteye at every opportunity, and I was losing weight because jet lag was killing my appetite. And I was getting more and more stressed out because Puff didn't seem too concerned about the deadline for the song, which he had delegated to me but was not giving any time to work on it.

"Let me talk to Puff, man," I said. "Maybe we can work something out."

"Forget it, Mark," Zack shot back. "The dude is rude to me and too full of himself. I've had it. I'm going back home."

After Zack left, I reflected on how differently Puff had treated him as compared to me. He treated me like I was his brother, but he treated my friend like he was the Invisible Man. He had wounded Zack's pride, even though Zack had more talent than many of the producers that worked for Bad Boy. I would make things right for Zack, but right now my hands were tied.

During a hiatus in the tour, I told Puff that I needed some place with privacy to stay if I was going to meet his deadline. The next morning, he sent a chauffeur for me. The driver took me to the Oakwood Apartments on Barham Boulevard in North Hollywood. Oakwood attracts scores of entertainers because it offers round-the-clock security to keep fans and stalkers out, and it's located within walking distance to Warner Bros Studios, Universal Studios, and Walt Disney Studios. All 1200 apartments are furnished, and it has rehearsal studios. It caters to the residents. Emma Thompson, Lou Gossett Jr., Aerosmith, and Queen Latifah have stayed there. Sometimes the studios book huge blocks of apartments for actors on films in production.

At Oakwood, I finally felt like I had arrived.

The deadline for the song was breathing down my neck. I asked for a clip of the scene where the song would be spliced in and watched it repeatedly. Then I thought about all those people running from the big celluloid green monster named Godzilla who had scared the hell out of me as a kid. And I thought about the heroes who always took him and other monsters out. I remember Puff's onstage mannerisms and how he moved, walked and talked in private.

All of a sudden, the lyrics started pouring out of my pen. By the next morning, I had written a song called "Come With Me," a song where the protagonist warns his enemies that he will end their lives if they mess with him, and a song that tells the people to follow me if they want to survive.

Puff loved it. "That's a hit like a muthafucka, Mark," he said after the first listen. "You a bad muthafucka!"

"That's a mean muthafucka," D-Mack added. He was smiling broadly now, realizing that he had just earned Brownie points with Puff and that his investment in me was about to pay off handsomely.

I expected that Puff would copyright the song in my name, pay me, and then send me home, but he had other plans. "I need you to stick around for a while, all right? I need you to rehearse the song with me and I need you to write some backup numbers in case the producers don't like the song as much as we do."

It sounded like an easy decision, but it wasn't. I loved Hollywood but I loved Deirdre more. I told Puff that I would have to talk to her first.

"That's cool, no problem," he said as he and D-Mack replayed the song. "You can bring her out here to live with you if you want to unless it'll fuck with your creativity."

"We also need to talk contract, though" I cautioned him. "I don't want to get into no legal hassles over my publishing rights with the movie's big shot lawyers."

"I got you covered, Mark," Puff assured me. "I'll protect you."

As I smirked, I wondered cynically what the hell he meant by that. Every time he "had me covered," I ended up holding the bag, usually one filled with overdue bills. But I let Puff take me out so far to sea on his dreamboat instead of my own that it was too late to turn back.

I called Deirdre and told her the good news about the song, but also had to tell her that I could not come home just yet. I felt like the road was hurting our relationship. However, if I give up now, I would have nothing in Atlanta. We'd be broke again and that's always bad for good relationships. As usual, she fully understood why I had to stay. We decided that she would visit me at least once a month until the stint was over.

A few days later, I rode with Puff to the Record Plant Recording Studios on Sycamore Avenue in Hollywood to record the song. It's among the most famous studios in modern music history. Everyone from John Lennon to Stevie Wonder to Kanye West has recorded there, and Jimi Hendrix had recorded at the one in New York. The studio brags that more Grammy-winning songs were recorded there than at any other studio in the world.

To get things rolling, I recorded the song first. My demonstration recording would be Puff's guide or reference point for the final product. From the outset, Puff struggled to convey the song's fury. He mispronounced words and put the emphasis in the wrong places.

When Sony's Artists and Repertoire (A&R) honchos came to the studio to see how things were going, Puff's jaws would get puffy-looking because every single one of them said that my version sounded so much better than Puff's version, and he got angry.

There was a rumor that two of the A&R people were even thinking of putting me under contract and having me record the song. I suspected that might have been true because all of a sudden, Puff wanted to rehearse with me night and day. He placed me on salary as his "vocal coach." He would watch me closely, then imitate every inflection, mannerism and hand gesture that I made as I performed the song for him. It was mimicry at its best. When you see Puff's performance in that video on the internet, you are seeing *me* perform that song.

Puff brought Bad Boy recording artist Mario Winans in to produce the song. After Jimmy Page re-recorded the guitar riffs, Winans overdubbed it on the original version of "Kashmir."

Although the movie bombed quickly after its release in May 1998, the soundtrack was a smash. Sony was moving more than 140,000 units a week by late May 1998. "The highest new entry on the singles chart this week is "Come With Me," *Music Week* wrote in its June 27 edition. "Page recreates some licks from Led Zeppelin's Kashmir, while Puff Daddy raps, and the result is a number 10 debut on the Hot 100."

"Come With Me" sold at three times the rate of the soundtrack. It was one of the most successful singles of the year, having scored triple platinum. I received the "Best Songwriter on a Soundtrack" prize at the annual ASCAP awards dinner.

I left Los Angeles for a while to go back to Atlanta. I missed Deirdre and my family. A few days after I returned, I was in the kitchen talking to my mother, my sister Diane, and Deirdre when the doorbell rang.

It was delivery man holding a rectangular box covered with a glittery gold foil wrapping paper.

"Oh, my God, Mark, what is it?" Mom asked. "Bring it here so we can all see!"

I hurried to the table and handed the package to my mother, who gently removed the wrapping. Inside was an expensive bottle of champagne. Mom picked up the note that came with the package and read it. "Brother Mark," it began, "Congratulations on the success of Come With Me." It was signed: "Puff and the Bad Boy Family."

Mom was so overwhelmed that she started crying. "I'm so proud of you!"

"I told you I'm gonna make it, Ma," I said as tears welled in my eyes. "And when I do, the first thing I'm gonna do is buy you a big house. I'm gonna take care of my whole family."

"Is that a promise?" my sister chimed in.

"Yeah, Diane. That's a promise."

CHAPTER 13

Slave Driver

Puff and I had increasing disagreements as the release of the "Godzilla" soundtrack approached. When D-Mack first called me about coming to LA, he said that Puff wanted to sign me to Bad Boy Entertainment. But once the song was completed, Puff refused to release it unless I signed a recording contract with D-Mack's new production company, Finish Line.

Although I was grateful to D-Mack for giving me a break, I had no desire to sign with his company for one main reason: the Finish Line contract required that I give half of all my publishing rights to

D-Mack for a pittance.

Based on marketing plans for the song and just plain ole common sense, I didn't want to sign the Finish Line contract since my publishing royalties had the potential to be worth millions. But Puff pressured me night and day, even suggesting that my recording career was over unless I signed the contract.

"Look Mark, we need to get this done. It's now or never," he said as I tried to read through all the legalistic mumbo-jumbo.

My confusion must have been obvious because Puff was smiling at me when I looked up from the stack of papers to ask him a question.

"Do you need a lawyer?" he asked.

"Yeah, man," I replied sullenly. "I'm gonna have to hire a lawyer to go over all of this with me."

"Damn, you don't trust me?" Puff said, again with a big toothy smile.

It's not that, Puff," I replied. "I just need to know what I'm getting into."

"Look, I tell you what. Since we're so short on time, I have a good friend that I send new artists to. Nobody has complained yet. He doesn't work for me so he won't bullshit you. He'll make sure that the contract is good."

He handed me the business card of Kenneth "Kenny" Meiselas, a lawyer with Grubman, Indursky, and Shindler. Puff rolled off a list of stars that the firm represented, among them Luther Van Dross, Billy Joel, David Geffen, Bruce Springsteen and Elton John. After he told me that, I figured that Meiselas would be cool, so I went to see him.

After a few minutes of flipping through it, Meiselas told me that the contract was kosher.

As I looked at the list of stars that the firm represented, I felt like Puff was giving me a square deal. Tommy Mattola, a friend of Puff's who made Maria Carey a superstar and then married her, also had close ties to the firm.

I knew that Puff was bluffing about not releasing the song, but I also knew that I could end up with nothing if the song was copyrighted without my name being on a contract, especially since everyone would assume that Puff wrote the song.

The implications of what I had signed didn't hit me until after my name was on the dotted line. In many ways, I was in the same spot as Biggie when he signed with Bad Boy. I was a poor cat who hadn't finished high school but I had musical talent. Puff was a rich cat with no musical talent but also with a stable of mostly white advisers and lawyers who taught him how to put voodoo on his artists.

After Biggie signed the contracts that Puff forced on him, for example, he walked away with only $25,000. To avoid people finding out just how broke Biggie was when he was killed, Puff announced that he was giving the fallen star's family several million dollars. If he had given Biggie a fair contract, Biggie would have had plenty of money to take care of his family forever and wouldn't have needed Puff's one-time charitable donation.

My contract called for a $75,000 advance. One third was a signing bonus, one third was for half of my publishing rights, and the last third would be given to me as soon as I finished my debut album. Since D-Mack's company took half of my publishing off the top, that left me with only $25,000.

The minute that I signed the contract, Puff bought it from D-Mack, so I asked him why didn't he just do a deal directly with me and do another deal with D-Mack.

"I have to take care of my friends," he answered. "D-Mack discovered you, so he had first rights to your contract." It all sounded like a noble gesture at the time, but I was too green to realize what was happening to me.

"Welcome to Bad Boy," Puff said grinning broadly, "where dreams come true." I smiled and thanked him even though I was baffled by what it all meant. I tried to hide my disappointment over the small amount of money actually going into my pocket, but I guess it must have been obvious.

I was in a foul mood for days after signing. I knew that I had been ripped off but I felt helpless. Puff tried to remove the edge off my anger by making me his protégé. After the soundtrack was finished and "Come With Me" won favorable reviews, he started teaming me up with other Bad Boy artists who were trying to break out. A few weeks after Biggie was murdered, I was in the Bad Boy studio working with a brilliant artist named Robert Ross, but better known as "Black Rob." We were working on the songs "Muscle Game" and "Down the Line" for his upcoming "Life Story" album.

Puff interrupted the session one day and said "Hey Mark, let's roll. Kim's having the baby!"

He had been dating Kim Porter for a couple of years. She was a former model who had just broken up with a famous R&B singer when Puff first laid eyes on her. I'm not sure what Kim had in mind for the baby's name, but Puff had been telling people for weeks that he was gonna name the baby after Biggie. On April 3, Kim gave birth to Christian Combs. Biggie's first name was Christopher, so I guess they reached some kind of compromise.

With his star gone, Puff was desperately searching for someone to replace Biggie. He initially hoped it would be Black Rob, but Rob was having legal troubles stemming from crimes he committed when he was homeless. After I wrote "Come with Me," Puff started banking on me to be the next big thing. He moved me into his old apartment in New York where he started Bad Boy.

They say that hindsight is 20-20, and that was certainly true in my case. I was so focused on making it that I didn't see any of the problems plaguing the Bad Boy team until I was on the roster.

I soon discovered that I wasn't the only artist who was getting burned by Puff. It turns out that most Bad Boy artists, including Biggie, had damn near the same contract, a deal that gave Puff half of everyone's publishing rights.

Nearly all of the artists were complaining about something, either being deprived of their royalties, creative differences in the studio, lack of promotion, or something. One of the most popular hip hop groups on the label, The Lox (short for "Living Off Xperience"), also had signed such a contract. Puff got half of their publishing.

The group, composed of three friends from the black ghetto in Yonkers, was fortunate enough in 1996 to get a demo tape to Mary J. Blige, who then recommended them to Puff. Puff immediately signed them to a six-album deal after listening to the tape, but refused to allocate a budget for the group. While telling them that they weren't polished enough for prime time, he took their best songs from the demo tape and recorded them for himself.

They had written "All About the Benjamins" and "I Got the Power," for their debut album. Not only did Puff take the songs for himself, but also added himself as one of the writers. He also claimed credit on their first independent hit, "We'll Always Love Big Poppa," which appeared on the flip side of "I'll Be Missing You."

"Poppa" and their two songs that Puff recorded garnered so much airplay that they felt certain that Puff would release their album by the end of 1997. Despite their begging, Puff refused to budge. Out of frustration, the trio got in touch with Steve Stoute of Interscope Records. Interscope wanted to help them get out of their contract with Bad Boy so it could release their work right away since they were hot.

As soon as Puff got wind of what was happening, he gave The Lox a budget and got them into the studio. Their first album, "Money, Power and Respect," was released in January 1998. Puff thought that he had pacified the trio, but he was mistaken. The album did well early on, but it sank fast because Puff failed to create a promotional program for the album and the group. The Lox was shocked when they discovered that their first publishing check was almost nothing.

They asked to be released from their contract because Puff and the lawyers that he had recommended had misled them and also because Puff wanted them to soften their "hard core" image. Again, Puff refused to budge. He told them that the contract was ironclad and that they owed him five more albums. To make matters worse, they were broke after splitting their small advance.

Seeing no other way out, The Lox had T-shirts made with "Free the Lox" stenciled on them. When they showed up at NBA games and concerts wearing the T-shirts, people wanted to know why they were wearing them. Once they explained, fans of the group had identical shirts made and before long, it was the latest fashion statement. All of the hip hop radio stations started asking about the merits of the group's charges against Puff.

Puff dodged questions about the group's royalties, but sensing that he had been outfoxed by the Lox, he released them from their future album obligations. However, he held onto his percentage of their publishing. The Lox soon signed a deal with Interscope, thinking that better days were ahead. They didn't find out until after their second album was released that Puff was still legally entitled to suck their publishing dry.

Mary J. Blige had been suckered into a similarly dirty contract when Puff brought her to Uptown Records. She was working her tail off and producing hits for Uptown, yet she had little or no money to show for it. Discouraged by events in her personal and professional life, Blige had started showing up inebriated at concerts because she felt like she was trapped.

When Suge Knight got out of jail and started Death Row, he heard about Blige's situation and the two of them talked about remedies. Suge learned that other major acts brought to Uptown by Puff were also being ripped off, including the singing group called Jodeci. Suge offered to get them out of their contracts if they agreed to let him manage their careers.

Although Suge and Puff were friendly at the time, the Blige incident ended their friendship. Suge told Puff in no uncertain terms that he was ripping off Blige, and that he wanted Puff to make things right. He understood that Suge was not asking him to do the right thing; he was demanding it. After a meeting with Puff and Uptown t executive and lawyer, Blige and Jodeci were released from their contracts without any compensation to Uptown.

Once we realized how badly Blige, Jodeci, Biggie and The Lox had been stiffed, we began worrying about our own publishing and careers. At the time, there were about eight artists besides me under contract: Carl Thomas, Faith Evans, Father MC, Total, Dream, Craig Mack, Black Rob and 112. He was afraid to mess with Faith, of course, because Biggie's fans would have killed him, but every other artists discovered that their careers would go nowhere as long as they were dancing with a devil called Puff.

Thomas was a gifted soul singer who joined Bad Boy's stable in

1997 after Puff saw him perform at a nightclub in New York City. He promised the 27-year-old crooner that his album would be out within a year. But once Thomas signed, Puff had him singing background vocals. And when BMG started asking Puff about the promised new material for a Biggie album, Puff remixed some unfinished songs by Biggie and dubbed in vocals by Thomas and some rhymes by me and other Bad Boy artists.

After nearly a year, Puff was still telling Thomas that he had to figure out a persona for him before releasing his album. It was only after constant complaining and writing a huge hit single that Thomas was able to get Puff to release it.

Black Rob was another artist who was getting burned. Puff signed Rob in 1996 and promised to release his album the following year. But like me, Thomas and The Lox, Black Rob spent the first year trying to write hits for Puff.

When I asked him what was holding up his album, Rob still had faith in Puff even though Puff knew he was in bad financial straits. He believed Puff when he said that his album was delayed by the death of Biggie. He believed Puff when he said that the birth of Christian Combs had interfered with the time block that he had initially set aside to work on the album. By the time Black Rob realized that Puff was just stonewalling, Puff's career had taken off and he couldn't catch Puff in the office or get him to answer phone calls.

When Black Rob started asking Puff to let him out of his contract, Puff finally started giving him studio time. The catch was that he was cooking the books to do so, engaging in a questionable practice called "piggybacking."

One night, for example, Mary J. Blige was doing a cameo for Bad Boy and was in the studio working with producer Stevie Jay for six hours straight. When the session was over, Stevie Jay and Blige left and dismissed the studio crew. But instead of letting everyone go home, Puff ordered the technicians and musicians to stay put. Then he called Black Rob and me into the studio and told us to work on a couple of songs for the next two hours.

When going over her accounts later, one of Blige's managers

asked her about the eight hours she was billed for studio time at Bad Boy. Blige told him that it was in error, and that she had worked six hours that night. Puff was confronted about the discrepancy and promised to look into it. He took so long that Blige ended up being billed anyway.

Once Puff realized that he wouldn't be able to siphon enough studio time to finish Black Rob's album, he reluctantly gave Black Rob a recording budget. Although the album went platinum, Puff had given him such a convoluted contract that Black Rob, a dropout with no job skills, was flat broke by the time it was released. To avoid the embarrassment of people finding out that he couldn't afford to pay child support with his meager publishing royalties from "Life Story," while Puff was living in luxury, Black Rob resorted to petty crime. Five months after his album dropped, he was serving time for burglary.

Being poor will do that to a man. You're young and confident and you see a golden opportunity, so you start signing stuff without recognizing that the devil is in the details.

Mase was in a similar predicament. Fortunately, Mase got so much media attention from his rhymes on the remix of "Only You" by Atlanta's 112 that everybody suddenly wanted him on their songs. Within six months, Mase had recorded with Mariah Carey, Brian McKnight, Busta Rhymes, and Puff, of course. Puff even dubbed Mase onto a couple of songs that Biggie had left in the vault.

Mase is the only Bad Boy artist I can recall whose album was released within a year of signing. In fact, it was partially the success of his quadruple-platinum "Harlem World" album in 1997 that prompted BMG to give Puff such a generous distribution deal.

CHAPTER 14

Mo' Problems

    In January 1998 Puff asked me to attend the American Music Awards with him. When I told him that I didn't have anything cool enough to wear, he took me to Bernini's clothing boutique on Rodeo Drive where I spent $5,000 on a suit, shirt, and Gucci shoes. Puff was up for five nominations that evening.

    He was certain that he'd win at least two awards for the music on his debut album, "No Way Out." He was up for Best Pop/Rock Male Artist against Beck and Babyface; Favorite Soul/R&B Artist against Babyface and Keith Sweat; Favorite Soul/R&B Album against Eryka

Badu, Mary J. Blige and Blackstreet; Favorite Soul/R&B New Artist against Dru Hill; Favorite Rap/Hip Hop Artist against Wu Tang Clan and Bone-Thugs-N-Harmony.

Puff knew that he didn't stand much of a chance against Badu, but he thought that he might win at least one or two awards. When he lost the first three nominations, he was still confident of the last two. But it was a shutout. Bone members stopped to acknowledge Puff, sitting on the end seat of the front row with his son Justin on his lap, as they headed for the stage.

Although he tried to keep up appearances by flashing a plastic smile, it was impossible for him to hide his hurt. "I'd be lying if I said I wasn't disappointed," he confessed as reporters surrounded him backstage after the show.

A few days later, Puff asked me to accompany him to the NBA All-Star game at Madison Square Garden. He was sponsoring an after-party where he planned to introduce me to a few players and music industry insiders, including his former mentor, Andre Harrell. Puff had just hired Harrell as President of Bad Boy. I soon discovered why.

After dropping out of Howard University in his sophomore year, Puff moved into the New Jersey mansion of Andre Harrell, founder of Uptown Records. Although his title was A&R, Puff was basically Harrell's Boy Friday. People teased him about having to carry an umbrella to keep the bachelor from melting in the rain.

The relationship was rocky from the start. Puff complained privately that Harrell treated him like his whore, and Harrell told people that Puff was too conniving and arrogant, making company decisions that were way above his "gopher" job duties. Harrell was supposedly looking for a way to fire Puff when Puff's concert blunder resulted in the trampling deaths of nearly a dozen teenagers. After the firestorm died down, Harrell fired Puff.

Puff was devastated. He went from being the fair-haired sidekick who spent weekends lounging by the pool to living in a dingy apartment in Harlem next to a thousand other nameless Harlemites. Because the deaths of the teenagers and Harrell's influence made Puff a pariah in the music industry, he was unable to find another music gig, so he decided to start his own label.

He was following in his mentor's footsteps, as Harrell started Uptown in 1987 after creative differences with Russell Simmons led him to quit Rush Management. At Rush, Harrell guided the careers of LL Cool J, Whodunit, and Russell's kid brother's group, Run DMC. Harrell accused Simmons of promoting a one-sided image of rappers, that of the hard-core gangster.

A former rapper himself, he was much more attuned to black culture than Simmons, and was too smart to stereotype all young black men as thugs. As part of the early 1980's duo called Dr. Jekyll and Mr. Hyde (his high school friend, Alonso Brown), Harrell had several hit records, among them "AM/FM, "Genius Rap," and "A Fast Life."

Unfortunately, fame went to Harrell's head. He went from being the humble son of a poor man to a multimillionaire in less than a decade. So he was justifiably proud, but unjustifiably arrogant. And as much as Puff despised him, he also worshiped him. They were two peas in a pod.

The Bible talks about the importance of treating people right because you never know when the tables will turn. In 1996, Harrell quit Uptown to become CEO of Motown, but his reign was a disaster and he "resigned" after only two years. When Puff heard that Harrell was out, he offered him a job as President of Bad Boy, which Harrell gladly accepted.

Puff remembered the humiliation he suffered under Harrell, and now it was payback time, or so people said. They said that Puff only hired Harrell in order to fire him. Within weeks of hiring Harrell, Puff started disrespecting him in public. They would be with a group of big shots when Puff would say something crude like "You wouldn't be shit without me" and "I made you and I can break you, nigga."

Harrell lived a lavish lifestyle, which was part of the reason that he fizzled so fast at Motown. Puff complained that Harrell had only taken the job offer because he needed the paycheck, and that he didn't really care about Bad Boy. That was the nature of their relationship when Puff introduced me to Harrell in February 1998, so you know the company was in trouble.

I was working on a new song in the studio a few days after the game when an excited secretary started tapping on the window. She was jumping up and down, laughing, and signaling me to come to her immediately. As I opened the door, she kept saying, "Congratulations, congratulations!"

I smiled and asked her for what, and she told me that I was receiving an ASCAP award for "Come With Me." I can't begin to describe how excited I was, but if you remember the first time you or your team won first place, then you know what I'm talking about.

Puff reserved a whole table for the ASCAP ceremony, but he kept giving me conflicting answers about whether he would attend. When I called him on the day of the event, he said that he couldn't make it. Although I was offended – I thought that he'd want to be there since it was a first for the Bad Boy label – the first time that one of his artists had made it big on a soundtrack, I wasn't going to miss the ceremony for anybody. I invited my friend Stef to go along, and he agreed.

Puff said that he was in the middle of launching his "Sean Jean" clothing line, which gave me an idea.

"Look," I said," since you can't make it, you should send me a few pieces from your collection to wear tonight."

"Damn, Mark, you're a genius!" he exclaimed. "I'll send a box of stuff over right now."

I showed up at the awards wearing a blue baseball cap and a white baseball jersey, both with "Sean John" embroidered on the front, and the jeans that I wore had his name sewn on them above the right pocket.

Although the theater was within walking distance of my hotel, Stef and I arrived late because the box of clothing didn't arrive until fifteen minutes before showtime. After showing the security guard at the entrance my identification, I told him that my name was on the table reserved for Sean Combs.

"That party hasn't arrived yet, Sir," the guard replied. "You'll have to wait in this area until Mr. Combs arrives."

"Where's the table?" I asked, hoping that someone seated there could come over and vouch for me. "I'm Mark Curry, one of the awardees."

He pointed to tables on the left side of the room. I didn't recognize anyone from Bad Boy at any of the tables, so I thought that he was mistaken at first. Then he said: "It's that empty table over there."

I couldn't believe it. One of the proudest moments of my life was taking place and I was on the outside looking in. I watched the stage as winners walked up and received their plaques and certificates. Everyone on the stage was white.

"Ladies and gentlemen," the announcer said, "the next award is for Best Songwriter on a Soundtrack. And the winner is . . . Mark Curry."

If the guard recognized my name, he didn't let on.

"Sir, you have to let me through! They're calling my name." The guard reiterated that rules prevented him from admitting me. As people in the crowd looked around to see who might be coming to the stage, Stef and I frantically waved our hands in the air.

"Yo', I'm back here!" I shouted, trying to attract the attention of Shari, the coordinator of the event. I pleaded with the guard to let her know that I was there. He put the walkie-talkie up to his mouth and radioed someone on stage to notify Shari of my presence.

By the time I received clearance, the announcers had moved on to the other awardees. Shari tried to cheer me up by telling me that I would still be able to participate in the photo opportunities afterward, and that those pictures would go on the international newswires.

I was somewhat disappointed, but what else could I do? The snafu illustrated why so many Bad Boy artists quickly grew disillusioned with the label and with Puff. Everything was a contest of wills with him. If he thought for one minute that you were trying to avoid becoming completely dependent upon him or that you were getting attention that he felt that he deserved, he would try to toss you aside or belittle you in some way.

For example, Biggie got mad about how Puff controlled his money and demanded a higher percentage once his career took off. Puff retaliated by threatening to sign more artists and to give less attention to promoting Biggie.

Once Biggie realized that everything with Puff was about the Benjamins, here's what he would do: He would let Puff arrange a series of concerts for him and pretend that everything was cool between them. But on the night of the concert, Biggie would go incommunicado and no one was able to find him. By the time Biggie showed up, it was ten minutes before showtime. Puff would damn near be on the verge of a heart attack. That's when Biggie would strike.

"Do we have a new deal or not?" Biggie would ask Puff as they waited backstage and the crowd screamed for the star. At that point, Puff would agree to almost anything.

Although I was flattered at first at how much Puff imitated me and depended upon me to teach him how to rap, other Bad Boy artists warned me that I was making a big mistake. They would tell me about what Puff did to a dude known as Sauce Money. Sauce Money (real name: Todd Gaither) was working with Jay-Z in mid-1970s. In fact, he's the cat who introduced Jay-Z to the business. He was featured on "Reasonable Doubt," Jay-Z's first album.

Jay-Z tried to get Sauce to sign with Roc-a-Fella, but Sauce was leery. He was in college at the time and a bit more astute than most rappers, and something about Damian Dash's business operations troubled him. However, the constant cheerleading of the label by Jay-Z after the success of his album finally convinced Sauce that the label was cool. Shortly after he signed, his apprehensions about Dash kept haunting him, and he left Roc-a-Fella after less than a year.

When Puff heard about this, he tried to lure Sauce to Bad Boy. At the time, Faith was trying to compose a song to commemorate Biggie's death but was too grief-stricken to focus. At the same time, dozens of writers were composing tributes to Biggie and sending them to Bad Boy. None of them seemed to interest Puff or Faith.

Sauce had already written a song using the Police's hit, "Every Breath You Take" as the sample and model. He had initially planned to sell it to Roc-a-Fella, but after Biggie was gunned down, he changed the words to his song, "I'll Be Missing You," and played it for Faith. She cried when he played it for her; she loved it.

The song was produced by Steven "Stevie-Jay" Jordan, one of a handful of producers called "The Hitmen" whom Puff shuffled between to prevent paying them fairly. (Another cat he used as a producer was Mario Winans). Everyone was surprised when the song debuted at the Number One spot on Billboard's Top 100 because no one realized that Biggie was idolized to that degree. It also quickly shot to the top of the charts in Canada, Europe and a dozen other countries. "I'll Be Missing You" went platinum sevenfold within months.

With the song making so much money, it was only a matter of time before some reporter got wind of the fact that most of the money was going to Puff. To avoid a dogfight with Biggie's mother over proceeds from the song, Puff told reporters that he was giving $3 million to Biggie's family.

Anxious to capitalize on the song's success, Puff added the song to an album that he was working on called "No Way Out." Typical of Puff's business practices at the time, however, was the fact that he released the song without getting permission from Sting and the Police, the copyright owners. Since the song made so much money, Arista was easily able to reach a settlement with Sting and his label.

Puff's "No Way Out" album had a couple of more hits on it, but the main reason for its success was pure and simple: Biggie. Biggie was featured on several cuts and Puff used samples from some of the biggest hits of the 1970s and 1980s. The album debuted at Billboard's Number One spot. It won the Grammy for best rap album of 1998, and *Rolling Stone* declared Puff the "Artist of the Year"

Puff was thrilled, of course, but Stevie Jay was fuming. He had long been fed up with how Puff was shortchanging him, so he took a page out of Biggie's playbook. This was during a period when Puff had hired Stevie Jay to work his magic with Mary J. Blige.

Puff and I were in LA having dinner one night when Stevie Jay called him. The producer had already put the finishing touches on a couple of songs for her, but Puff was putting pressure on him to produce more.

"What you've got is nice, but it ain't Top Ten. I need you to produce a couple of more, make a couple of more efforts."

"You haven't paid me a dime, Puff," Stevie Jay shot back. "I'm up here working my ass off and you got a big-ass budget for Mary J, but you don't wanna do right by me, man. You gonna have to come up with some money fast or I'm walkin'."

"You're treating me like you're my bitch or something," Puff replied. It was cheap shot that he calculated would make Stevie Jay back off, but it backfired.

"I may not be your bitch," Stevie Jay said, "but I'm the man who puts the fur coat on your bitch's back and the ring on your bitch's finger. You better stop fucking with my money or you won't get shit. I want $300,000 now or I'm outta here." With that, Stevie Jay hung up the phone and refused to answer any more calls from Puff.

Stevie Jay didn't show up at Bad Boy studios the next day and Mary J. Blige was ticked off. She was stuck in the middle of somebody else's mess, but she knew how trifling Puff was when it came to money so she didn't aim her anger at Stevie Jay.

Puff had several people in the office plead with Stevie Jay to call him, but he ignored them. Then one of Puff's assistants told Stevie Jay that Puff was willing to give him $30,000 immediately.

Stevie Jay called Puff and told him that he was crazy to think he could get all of those songs for so little money. "I won't finish the project for less than $300,000," he said. Puff pleaded with him, claiming that he had nowhere near that kind of money, but he doubled his offer to $60,000. He also promised him a bonus if any of the songs went to the top of Billboard.

Stevie Jay knew from the start that he would not get $300,000. But he had also learned that it was impossible to get anything close to a fair shake with Puff unless your original demand was astronomical. That's the way Puff dealt with the studios, and that was the only type of deal-making that he seemed to respect.

Stevie Jay took the second offer, but things were never the same between them because the producer felt that Puff had played him and paid him cheap. He lured him in with promises of big money and dividends, and then tried to get hit songs at slave labor wages.

CHAPTER 15

Losin' It

Things really took off for Puff the Rapper after *Rolling Stone* put him on the cover issue in August 1997. The cover mentioned the deadly fall of Biggie and Tupac and the rise of Puff as the "new king of hip hop."

The article was written by Mikal Gilmore, the younger brother of two-bit killer Gary Gilmore. Sensing that Puff was hot, Ballantine Books gave them a $350,000 advance for an autobiography to be ghost-written by Gilmore and ready for publication within one year.

With bonuses from recent successes at Bad Boy, Puff was getting between $40 and $65 million from BMG, and about $20 million of that was a bonus just for Puff. On top of that, the Sean John clothing line was raking in millions.

While all of the media attention was good news for Puff, it was bad news for me and other Bad Boy artists. Puff was so consumed with the Bad Boy clothing line and his own career as a rapper that we had trouble getting the time of day from him.

Because he has so little trust in other people, every document involving the company had to be reviewed by him before any action could be taken, and he was too busy to look at anything.

Puff would get so wired sometimes – his favorites were weed, ecstasy and xannies (Xanax) – that he wouldn't realize that he was speeding. Puff, Kim told *Newsweek,* was getting by on only "two or three hours of sleep" and had been doing so for years.

Friends had nicknamed him "Vampire" because he was up all night. But while he's speeding, he's burning other people out because almost no one has that amount of energy naturally. He was keeping a pace that was unnatural, and he actually rhymed about the effect that the drugs were having on him. In the song, "Do You Like It?" he asked:

> *Where do you go from here when you've felt you've done it all*
> *When what used to get you high don't get you high no more?*

He was about to find out.

Puff started exploiting Mase in the same way that he was exploiting Biggie, forcing the brother's sound on any artist who would have him. By early 1999, when he was pressuring Mase to complete his second album, he also lent Mase out to over a dozen other record labels at the same time. Mase recorded with Brandy, Jay-Z, Monifah and almost everything that Bad Boy released.

When Mase got busted in 1998, it dawned on him that he had fallen for the hype about hip hop. He wasn't the hard-core thug that he rapped about, and he was smart enough to realize that young dudes were trying to do the things that he rapped about. Being incarcerated opened Mase's eyes just like it does for a lot of young cats.

The second revelation for Mase came in April 1999. Puff had been working with a new artist known as Nas (real name: Nasir Jones), a grade school dropout who self-schooled himself by studying mysticism and the Bible, and who learned about Islam from his father, a popular jazz musician.

While working on a double album to be released by Stoute on Interscope, Nas and Puff came up with the idea of a video for a single called "Hate Me Now." Puff was so self-absorbed at the time that he started acting like he was an invincible, messianic figure. Hype Williams, a successful video director, shot a scene in which Nas and Puff were crucified in the same manner as Jesus Christ.

The video caused friction between Puff and some of his artists, especially me and Mase, as we sat on the set and watched an early version. Mase had been quietly studying the Bible with Foxy Brown, another up-and-coming artist who was very religious. "Rap music is the devil," he began telling her after seeing the video. He told her that he was going to abandon hip hop and start preaching the gospel, and he urged her to do the same. Brown listened but felt that Mase was losing his grip on reality.

When Columbia Records gave Puff a copy of the video on April 11, he showed it to his mother and to his pastor, the Rev. Hezekiah Walker. They told him that the video was blasphemous, and Walker asked Puff point blank what he was thinking when he agreed to be part of it.

Mase and I had told him the same thing days earlier, but Puff was too distracted to listen. By the time he straightened up enough to get his mother's opinion, it was too late.

On April 15, Puff called Stoute and told him that he had reconsidered the video and wanted it destroyed before someone got hold of it. Stoute told him that the video had already been released to several video channels and it would be impossible to retrieve it. Within hours of the conversation, the video aired on MTV.

Puff became hysterical as we watched the video at Bad Boy. He saw how foolish they both looked by comparing themselves to Christ. Even the "yes men" and women in the office looked at Puff like he had lost his mind.

"Oh, my God," several staffers said as they watched in disbelief.

"That's going to ruin him," someone whispered.

Puff's jaws filled with air, his eyes got bigger and watery, and you could see his temple throbbing. He turned the TV off and started to harangue us.

"This is war!" he yelled. "We need to go over there and teach that nigga that he's messing with the wrong niggas! Who's with me?"

Paul "Ox" Oxford, one of Puff's main bodyguards, was one of the first to volunteer.

Puff kept talking, trying to get more backers. He stared at D-Mack, so D-Mack reluctantly agreed to go with them. But for the most part, the rest of us knew that Puff was acting unstably and probably was about to do something to get his ass locked up, so none of us stepped forward.

"Y'all just a bunch of bitch-ass pussies," he yelled as the three of them left the building.

They headed straight over to Stoute's office in the Universal Music Group building. Interscope was a subsidiary of Universal, which was a subsidiary of the multinational Seagram Company. That was another reason no one else volunteered. Puff was acting like he was dealing with some chicken-shit operation instead of one of the largest companies in the world. I was already on probation. Plus, I had told him before he even shot that shit that it was a lame idea.

Puff, Ox, and D-Mack barged past the front desk at Universal and went directly to Stoute's office. Although Stoute was in a meeting with two colleagues, Puff ordered them to leave as he walked toward Stoute's desk and turned it over on him. As Stoute fell to the floor, he held the phone in his hand and tried to call police.

Puff snatched the phone from Stoute and started hitting him on the head with it. As Puff beat him with the phone, Ox and D-Mack punched and kicked Stoute. Ox grabbed a chair and threw it at Stoute. Then Puff grabbed an empty champagne bottle and struck Stoute in the face. As blood dripped from Stoute's head and face, Ox signaled that it was time to leave before the police arrived. They trashed the office and ran off.

Stoute was rushed to St. Clare's Hospital by colleagues who heard the ruckus as it was ending. After being treated for his wounds, he gave the police a statement. He told them that the only assailant he knew was Puff, but that there was a bodyguard with him that he had seen before, and that one of the men was referred to as "D-Mack."

The night after the attack, a group of us from Bad Boy accompanied Puff to a party for the launching of *Notorious,* his new magazine. When a reporter asked Puff whether he was involved in the alleged attack, he gave a bizarre answer: "Not to my knowledge," he said. And when questioned by police, Puff initially denied knowing anything about the attack. He later told reporters who had gotten wind of the brazen assault that it was probably a case of mistaken identity, and that he was innocent.

When a reporter mentioned that police had possession of video from a security camera showing him and several other men entering Universal's building, Puff changed his story. He claimed that he had gone to see Stoute, and that the two got into a fistfight over the video.

After consulting with his lawyers, Puff turned himself in. He was booked on felony assault and criminal mischief charges. Since he had a prior "violation" (he was charged with assault and criminal mischief in 1996 after pulling a gun on a *New York Post* photographer), bail was set at $15,000.

Russell Simmons of Def Jam told reporters what everybody around Puff was thinking, including me. "He was worried about being on a cross, but he's on a corporate cross now," Simmons said. "It's going to be a costly lesson for him."

Ox turned himself in on April 20 after recognizing that they had made a huge mistake in attacking Stoute. The issue had blown up so much that Edgar Bronfman Jr., president of Seagram, was involved. Bronfman called Stoute personally to "apologize on behalf of the corporation." While the New York Police Department issued a statement saying they were still pursuing the third suspect, D-Mack quietly flew back to Los Angeles to lay low for a while. Someone told *Los Angeles*

Times investigative reporter Chuck Phillips that the third suspect was known as "D-Mack," and the *LAT* was the only major paper to report that scoop.

A few days before trial, Puff called Stoute to apologize and pleaded with him to drop the charges. Puff had good reason to beg: if he was convicted, he would face a maximum of seven years' incarceration.

Stoute agreed, but advised Puff that he still planned to file a civil action. Puff was used to paying his way out of messes, so that was a no-brainer. He just didn't want to do any jail time. They settled a civil suit with Stoute reportedly receiving close to a half million dollars.

As part of a plea deal, the charge was reduced to a "harassment violation," meaning that Puff would not have a criminal record. The deal also meant that instead of facing serious time in jail, Puff was sentenced to a one-day class in anger management.

Oddly, Stoute hired Jacques "Haitian Jack" Agnant as part of his security team after the attack. Agnant had once been allied with Puff.

Stoute wasn't the only friend whom Puff had crossed in recent weeks. Benny Medina, his personal manager, also parted ways with Puff. When asked about the split, a close friend of Medina's said that it "takes a lot of work to work with Puffy." Medina was the dude whose life story was the basis of the hit TV series, "The Fresh Prince of Bel-air," starring Will Smith. In addition to co-producing the show, he was also a heavyweight in the Warner Bros. music division.

Even though Puff and Stoute kissed and made up, an internal investigation was launched by BMG. Executives at its headquarters in Germany began questioning why Clive Davis, head of Arista Records, offered someone so unprofessional the $50 million advance that he had given Puff. Davis replied that Bad Boy had earned over $130 million in 1998 and that the advance was a good investment. Davis assured BMG that Puff's advisors would keep Puff in check.

By the nature of the questioning, however, Davis knew that his days at Arista were numbered. BMG didn't want to be bothered with someone crazy enough to do what Puff did to Stoute. But besides that, the company was looking for a reason to fire Davis, the founder of Arista, because he was rumored to be still engaging in unethical practices to promote his artists and also because he simply had amassed too much influence over the music feeding chain over the past 30 years.

BMG reminded Davis that what Puff had done to Stoute constituted a "material breach" of their contract. If Puff was convicted, or if there was another criminal incident involving Puff or his artists, BMG said, Puff was toast. Since Davis was backing him up, he knew that his career would be over if Puff ever did anything else that stupid.

After talking to Davis about BMG's threat, Puff went before reporters to feign remorse. "I am embarrassed," Puff said. "That's not me. I disappointed my fans, my family, and I disappointed hip-hop." No one thought to ask him why he felt it was not him assaulting Stoute. And if it wasn't him, who the hell was it?

Once again, Puff had gotten off too easily. Each time he got in trouble, hotshot lawyers got him off the hook. Bill Kunstler got him off the hook in 1991 when the kids got trampled to death, when he could have been charged with involuntary manslaughter. Although Puff had tried to pay the families next to nothing, some of the parents refused to settle.

Four months before the Stoute incident, a New York judged ruled that the City College of New York, Puff and Heavy-D were jointly responsible for the deaths of nine kids.

Judge Louis Benza basically called Puff a liar for claiming that he stayed with the dead and injured kids until help arrived. He noted that several witnesses testified that they saw Puff "standing there with two women, and all three had money [bags] in their hands." He also condemned Puff for claiming that he had no idea that the event might turn deadly.

"It does not take an Einstein to know that young people . . . who have paid as much as $20 a ticket, would not be very happy and easy to control if they were unable to gain admission to the event because it was oversold." And he reminded the public again that Puff had sold more than 5,000 tickets for a gymnasium with a maximum capacity of half that number.

Parents of the dead children publicly castigated Puff and Heavy-

D for fighting so hard and for so many years to avoid paying for the pain that they caused. A lawyer for the families said that they could not understand how a rich young black man could be so greedy and selfish.

"Nine African Americans died," he said. "Sean Combs is an African American. A large portion of his income and wealth is derived from people of color. That being the case . . . I think he should have demonstrated a greater willingness to come forth with the money."

Johnnie Cochran got him off the hook when he threatened the photographer and Harvey Slovis got him out of the scrape with Stoute. Since there seemed to be no real consequences to his actions, Puff kept on misbehavin' and doing stuff that most CEOs would never do in their worst nightmares.

CHAPTER 16

Breakdown

On August 10 – just four months after the Stoute incident – Puff was still acting like he was jacked up on a steroids and bennies cocktail. One of his first stops of a national tour to promote his second album, "Forever," was Detroit's leading hip-hop radio station WCHB-FM.

His publicist, Lisa Spiritus, had contacted Dr. Roger Mills, a devout Christian who had a locally popular program focusing on celebrities and faith, to see whether he was interested in having Puff do a segment for his show while he was there.

Dr. Mills said yes, and told her that he would set up his equipment inside the station for an interview immediately following the WHCB-FM interview. After Puff introduced himself and told Dr. Mills how much he had changed and renewed his faith in Jesus since the attack on Stoute, the interview began. In the course of the interview, Mills asked Puff to comment on recent allegations that he was somehow involved in Biggie's murder.

"This shit is over!" Puff yelled. He threw off the headphones and walked out of the station. Puff's bodyguards gave menacing looks to Mills who began to fear for his safety. As he packed up the digital recording equipment, Spiritus approached him and asked how much he wanted for the videotape. "Money is no object," she said.

Mills explained that he couldn't sell the tape because it was a master copy containing a host of other celebrity interviews, and that he had no backup copy since the camera was on loan to him. Mills and his producer then left the building and headed for his Jeep Wrangler on the parking lot.

As they entered the jeep, Puff's bodyguards and others in the group attacked them. Someone grabbed the camera, ripped out the videotape and smashed the camera. After damaging the jeep, they sped away in Lincoln Navigators.

Mills immediately drove to a local police station to file a complaint. News reports about the incident were on the air within hours, as Mills was highly regarded in Detroit.

In the days after the incident, Mills noticed that he was being stalked, usually by black men in black Lincoln Navigators. He was also getting harassing phone calls from someone claiming to represent Puff. After the calls started, Mills had a surveillance system installed inside and outside of his home. The stalking suddenly stopped.

Two weeks later – August 24 – Puff flew to San Francisco. He was uncomfortable about being in public on the West Coast after Tupac and Biggie got killed. A lot of people spread rumors that he and Suge were involved in their deaths because both had profited handsomely after their leading artists were murdered.

Artists on the West Coast were also angry with Puff because they believed that BMG and other companies financing Puff and Def Jam used payola to keep stations from playing videos and music by West Coast hip-hop artists.

The interviews were going fine until Puff stopped by KYLD-FM for an interview with two white disc jockeys known as Elvis and J.V., hosts of the "Dog House." J.V. brought up the topic of East Coast-West Coast rivalry. Biggie had done a live interview with J.V. three days before he died. He said on the air that he was fearful of being murdered because of all the East Coast-West Coast tension (the video-tape of the interview is still on Youtube).

That was another reason that Puff was uncomfortable being there and discussing violence. In fact, when he set the ground rules for inter-views during the tour, one of them was that there could be no ques-tions about the rivalry, the death of Biggie, or anything except the album.

Puff's jaws filled and released air like a blowfish when J.V. dis-agreed with his contention that the conflict was over. Then Puff lost it.

"You muthafuckin' clown! What the fuck do you think you're do-ing bringing that shit up? Don't you know that's how shit gets started?"

J.V. got visibly nervous as Puff continued yelling at him on the air. The bodyguards moved in closer to Puff, hoping to calm him down. The station broke for commercials while it tried to restore or-der.

After the break, J.V. asked his callers if they had any questions for Puff because he was done. He also said that he was sorry for riling Puff, but that he thought he asked a fair question.

"You a hater," Puff yelled before the station even took the first call. "I better get the fuck out of here before I start whipping some ass!"

As Puff threw off his headphones, Ox and other security guards grabbed the video camera that was capturing the interview and ripped the film out.

J.V. said that Puffy was way out of line, had misunderstood the intentions of his questioning, "has too big a head" and had hurt his stature with local fans.

"It was the biggest PR blunder he could have made," the disc jockey said a little later. "We got hundreds of calls and e-mails, and nearly every one of them was down on Puffy. They hate his guts out here now. He really blew it."

It didn't matter, though, because the interview was on audiotape, a copy of which undoubtedly found its way back to BMG. Puff's antics had now resulted in another strike against Clive Davis, the man who made Puff wealthy.

It wasn't just Davis, Bad Boy artists, and the poor, uneducated hip hop artists like me who were getting burned by Puff's crazinesss. He had been spending money so fast since Biggie's death that he seemed to be robbing Peter to pay Paul. One of the biggest scams he ran was against Arista and Clive Davis, the hand that was feeding him.

Part of the reason that Davis gave Puff the $50 million contract was because Puff promised to produce a collection of unpublished songs from Biggie and a gospel album that would shake up the world of black music. He promised to release the gospel album in 1996.

Among the artists in the lineup were Vickie and Mario Winans of the famous family, the Reverend Hezekiah Walker, Brian McKnight, Faith Evans, Brandy, Carl Thomas and the duo Mary Mary.

Puff allegedly allocated several million dollars for the album, including half a million dollars in studio time – then spent most of it on something else. He was pouring money into the Sean John clothing line, the rapidly failing *Notorious* magazine, new jewelry, cars and other pet projects.

He bought a condominium in New York one floor above Tony Mottola, and used a corporation that he owned to buy a house in the Hamptons. When Arista asked about the progress of the album, Puff kept giving them excuses. At first he attributed part of the delay to his decision to include songs by two new Bad Boy artists who sang gospel music. One was a gifted young woman named Tanya Blount and the other a 12-year-old prodigy known as "Li'l Jerome.

Several songs from the album were completed by 1998, but the full album never got the production nod. That was the first and last time that Puff tried to venture into gospel music. Nearly every artist on the planned album had left Bad Boy by the time Puff set a release date.

The loss of so many artists and the loss of Benny Medina as his mentor were two of Puff's biggest setbacks after he took on the dual role of rapper and record mogul. The biggest setback by far, however, was the end of his friendship with Kirk Burrowes, cofounder of Bad Boy Entertainment.

Burrowes was a rising star at Orion Pictures when Andre Harrell approached him about joining Uptown Records. His marketing management skills had placed him on the fast track at Orion, but Burrowes found the challenge of turning a no-name upstart black-owned company into a multimillion dollar company an irresistible lure, so he signed on in 1992.

His skills made Heavy-D and several other Uptown artist superstars. When Harrell fired Puff, they both fought over Burrowes. Burrowes, who was managing Mary J. Blige at the time of the split, placed his bets with Puff since Puff offered him twenty-five percent of Bad Boy. The two became such good friends that Puff asked Burrowes to be the godfather of his first child, Justin.

One of the first things that Burrowes did was to hire a staff of competent young African American professionals to run Bad Boy. Even though the public thinks that Puff's production skills made Biggie a superstar, it was in fact Burrowes who spearheaded the rise of Bad Boy's first superstars.

When the East Coast-West Coast rift developed in 1995, it was Burrowes who secured a record deal for Brooklyn vocalist Kim Summerson with Aftermath Records, founded by Dr. Dre. Burrowes said that the deal was intended to lessen tensions between the emerging black companies on either coast.

"Kirk is the one responsible for Bad Boy's success and making it the professional, young, black-run company that it has become," Puff told reporters in early 1997. The press conference was made to announce that Puff was promoting Burrowes from general manager to president of Bad Boy Entertainment.

The statement was true, and future events would show that Bad Boy was nothing without Burrowes at the helm. But Burrowes would soon charge that Puff had hidden motives when he made that announcement.

According to Burrowes, once Medina became Puff's mentor and Arista started throwing money at Bad Boy, Puff decided to get rid of him because he was entitled to one-fourth of Bad Boy Entertainment's profits.

Several months before Puff made the announcement praising him, Burrowes said that Puff and Kenny Meiselas came into his office one afternoon and that Puff was carrying a baseball bat. As Meiselas looked on, Burrowes said, Puff forced him to sign over his twenty-five percent stake in the company.

Puff told Burrowes that if he didn't sign the contract, his management of Mary J. Blige's career would come to an abrupt end. Thirdly, he threatened to blackball Burrowes so no one else would hire him.

The glowing comments at the press conference were apparently intended to prevent Burrowes from going public with the shakedown. Puff quietly removed the formerly "indispensable" Burrowes from managing Bad Boy and replaced him with Andre Harrell.

Fearing for his life, Burrowes signed the contracts and left Bad Boy Entertainment, hoping that would be the end of the matter. He formed his own company, Kirk Burrowes Entertainment, and continued to manage Blige's career.

When staff members heard about how Puff had disrespected Burrowes, most of them concluded that if the man who made Puff rich meant nothing to him, they probably mattered even less.

By the end of 1998, two of the most popular artists at Bad Boy were threatening to join the exit began by The Lox. The Atlanta-based group 112 said that they would leave the label unless Puff gave them more creative control on their second album.

With Puff taking production, writing, and copyright credits from them on their debut album, the trio saw little money. After months of haggling, Puff relented.

He was not so successful with the other rebellious artist, Mase. Born in Jacksonville, Mase's family moved to Harlem when he was 5. When he was 13, his parents sent him back to Florida because he was running with the wrong crowd. Two years later, he returned to New York to play basketball and to chase his dreams of one day becoming a rapper. He called himself "Murda Mase."

He was a part of a rap group called Children of the Corn. The Children of the Corn started out as neighborhood acquaintances. It included Mase, Killa Kam, Bloodshed, and Big L.

Unable to garner much attention, the Harlem rappers soon dispersed and Mase decided to go solo. In 1996, he went to Atlanta for the "Jack the Rapper Convention" with hopes of hooking up with Jermaine Dupri; instead, he met Puff. Puff was blown away by Mase's laid-back style, and quickly signed him to Bad Boy Records. He was a slick-rhyming, diamond-flaunting, skirt-chasing player, no doubt about it. Women loved him.

Mase wanted to dress in videos just as he dressed in everyday life, but a lot of record companies were trying to make their artist mimic the sartorial styles of MC Hammer and Vanilla Ice. Puff was no exception. Over Mase's objections, Puff put him in shiny suits that ended up damaging the young man's street credibility. And it didn't help his credibility at all to be seen dancing and kicking it with Puff in every video.

I first met him on the "No Way Out" tour. He was good-spirited and humorous at first, but gradually became more introspective. One day, he told us that he felt like God was speaking to him, and he had a vision that the phony lifestyle projected in his music and videos was leading millions of young people to Hell. He rattled some reporters during the tour by blurting random religious sayings at them.

"Come back and see me at the God Hour," he kept yelling. We had to tell him to chill, but when a man is going through something like that, it's hard to reason with him.

By the time his second album was released, Mase felt like he couldn't go on preaching one thing and believing the opposite. The video of Puff playing Jesus left him with the impression that Puff would do anything to make a buck, that he would exploit the murder of Jesus Christ as easily and as quickly as he exploited the murder of Biggie Smalls.

He shocked fans by saying during a radio interview that the devil was trying to buy his soul, and it wasn't for sale. He told Puff that he would not promote the album because it conflicted with his newfound faith, and that he was planning to leave music and preach the gospel of Jesus Christ. Despite threats of legal action from Puff, Mase refused to promote the album and it bombed fast. It was one of the first times that I witnessed Puff get burned by his own fire.

After leaving Bad Boy and its "devil music," Mase joined the ministry. Pastor Mason Betha spent the next several years establishing S.A.N.E. (Saving A Nation Endangered) Church International, a multicultural, nondenominational house of worship with roughly 2,000 members, he says. Videos of his sermons are on the internet.

With the departure of The Lox and Mase, Bad Boy was left with three artists with whom Puff hoped to make as much money from as he had with Biggie: me, Black Rob, and the new kid on the block, Jamal "Shyne" Barrow.

Kenneth Curry (my father) and his close friend formed one the early integrated rock 'n' roll groups in America.

JOHNNIE & JOE
Exclusively on
J & S Records

Management:
Sprout Enterprises
N.Y.C.

My father's first wife was Johnnie Richardson of the famous
"Johnnie and Joe" duo. Johnnie's mother was Zelma "Zell"
Sanders, one of the first black women to own a record label.

My father's winning looks, personality, and silky-smooth voice made him a hit with the ladies.

A live holiday performance at age 2 with Tina and Monte.

SENSATIONAL WILLIAMS BROS.
OF SMITHDALE, MISS. RFD 1, BOX 67

I was baptized in 1983 after moving to Mississippi to live with my brother. I discovered that our family had a rich gospel music legacy, including the "Sensational Williams Brothers."

People laughed when Dad bought this run down shack . . .

. . . and stopped when he turned it into the best-looking house in the community.

Kenneth Curry opened Rockin' Robin's Record Shop and
Currison's after forsaking a career as a recording artist.

Charlie, Chris and I perform as "The Breaking Sensations" in junior high school in Teaneck.

The Metro Section

The New York Times

No Liability Insurance at Game That Led to the Deaths of 9

More Paid for Publicity Than Security at Event, Sponsor's Lawyer Says

By ROBERT D. McFADDEN

Blame for the charity basketball game at which nine people were fatally crushed at City College last weekend went around and around again yesterday amid disclosures that the event was produced with an unusual contract, with no liability insurance and with a budget that spent far more on promotion than on security.

Lawyers for the promoters and officials of the City University said that the brief contract to produce the event made a student group responsible for what proved to be inadequate security, made promoters responsible for insurance that was never obtained, and did not include the college — ordinarily responsible for all events on campus — even as a party to the agreement.

On a day of investigatory sessions, news conferences, interviews and statements, the only real point of agreement was the sense of needless tragedy about the deaths at Jeremiah T. Mahoney Hall last Saturday night — and the consistent disclaimers of responsibility by all parties.

"We don't throw functions for people to get killed or to be injured," Dwight Meyers, the rap star known as Heavy D. who helped organize the game said at a news conference in an ornate room at the Plaza Hotel. "We throw functions to make money to raise money and for people to have fun."

William M. Kunstler, Heavy D's lawyer acknowledged that the promoters had not obtained liability insurance, but he brushed aside questions on why, and insisted that City College officials should have been responsible to make sure adequate security and proper insurance were in place.

And Mr. Kunstler insisted that the promoters were young and inexperienced, perhaps not as diligent as they might have

Many news conferences and denials of responsibility.

been, but people who were simply trying to do a good thing for charity.

Witnesses have said the crush occurred when a crowd of more than 2,000 people funneling into an already crowded gym surged forward pressing those ahead. The pressure moved through the crowd down a stairway and into a well in front of a single door that was open for ticketholders. There, out of sight of the mass of humanity pressing from above, victims were buried and smothered.

At one news conference yesterday, the promoters and their lawyers accused the police, the Emergency Medical Service and the college of mishandling various aspects of the affair. At another news conference, the nation of Islam, which had been identified as one of the groups that had provided security, denied any role whatsoever.

A City University official, in an interview, acknowledged that City College officials might have been more aggressive in obtain-

"We don't throw functions for people to get killed or to be injured," said Dwight Meyers, the rap star known as Heavy D, as he spoke at a news conference about the deaths at City College. Next to him was Sean Combs, a promoter of the event.

ing proof of insurance and checking on other arrangements. And a lawyer for the student government leader who signed the contract said he believed she would not face criminal charges.

With potentially heavy criminal and civil liabilities at stake, the voices of accusation appeared to be growing more strident. And the lack of insurance suggested that heavy burdens might fall on those ultimately found responsible. That circle could include the state as the fiscal and legal parent of the City University, the city through its police and medical personnel, the event's promoters and various security groups.

As investigations by City Hall, the City University and Manhattan's District Attorney continued five days after the tragedy, charges swirled around planning and security arrangements for what was to have been a basketball game featuring celebrity rap stars.

But but there was no new light shed on a crucial question: What ignited the stampede of pushing and shoving that moved like a human wave through the crowd outside the gym at 138th Street and Convent Avenue and left nine young people fatally injured at the bottom of a stairway leading to the gym doors.

In an interview, Mr. Kunstler disclosed that the $58,000 expense budget for the game had included as its largest item $2,200 for advertising on KISS-FM, radio station WRKS, which heavily promoted the game, especially in the hours before it was held.

Continued on Page 8

At a wake yesterday in New Rochelle, N.Y., for Sonya Williams, one of the victims of the crush at City College, a woman consoled a young girl.

Puff hides his face in shame as Dwight "Heavy D" Myers addresses the media about the celebrity basketball game at City College where nine children were trampled to death in 1991.

Partying at Platinum House in 1995 with James the Soundman (in white short sleeves) and my main man Baby Looney.

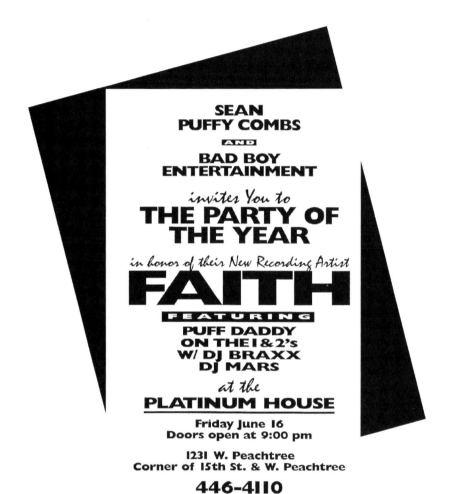

A Platinum House flyer announcing the release of the debut album by Faith Evans. Platinum House got off to a royal start but ran into trouble after Puff's bodyguard killed "Big Jake" Robles two days after Robles was released from prison. Robles was a close personal friend and bodyguard to Suge Knight.

Me, crazy Jay-D (with cigarette) and friends at the Million Man March in October 1995.

Taking five with Li'l Cease (in Dodgers jersey) and Junior M.A.F.I.A. friends a few years ago. Cease reveals in an explosive documentary how Puff abandoned Notorious B.I.G. just hours after Biggie was gunned down.

Mark Jr. and I pose with Voletta Wallace at a book signing in Atlanta

Puff, D-Mack (in white cap) and I celebrate after I became a
Bad Boy artist (months after the murder of Notorious B.I.G).
Puff told a grand jury during the Shyne Trial four years later
that he did not know D-Mack's real name.

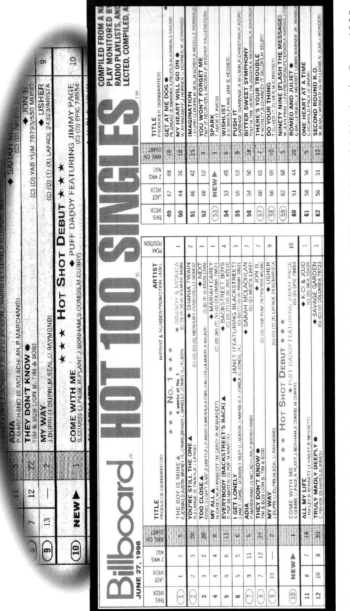

The first song that I wrote for Puff shot to the top of the Billboard Hot 100 Singles in June 1998. "Come With Me" was also the first song by a Bad Boy artist to be featured in a movie. My cousin Brandy had the number one single the same week.

Celebrating my 1998 win of an ASCAP award for "Come With
Me," with Shari and my close friend Stef.

Puff asked Biggie to teach
him how to be a rapper
shortly before Biggie was
murdered. After he signed
me to Bad Boy, Puff made
the same request of me.

Out on the town in South Beach with Jennifer "J-Lo" Lopez and Puff.

-- People

Burning the midnight oil in the Bahamas after the "No Way Out" tour.

Police who arrested Puff and Shyne on December 27, 1999 recall Puff urging his chauffer Fenderson and bodyguard Anthony "Wolf" Jones to claim ownership of a gun found in the car near Puff's feet.

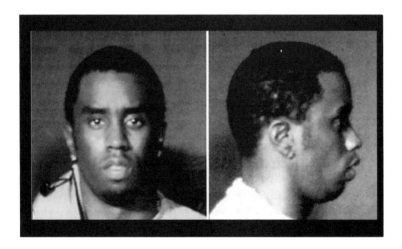

Puff was also accused of trying to bribe witnesses to the club shooting two days after Christmas.

Puff, Black Rob and me from the cover of a hit that I wrote
with Morock of the Hoodfellas.

The wonders of modern technology allowed Puff to continue
making money from the slain rapper Notorious B.I.G.

The cover of *The Source* featuring the Bad Boys, and in the background, the World Trade Center towers. That's me in the far left hand corner.
-- *The Source*

Recording poetry for "The Saga Continues" in Miami.

Getting my party on en route to Morocco in 2002.

Performing at MTV's HIV/AIDS Awareness concert in Capetown in November 2002.

My good friend and fellow Bad Boy artist Craig Mack (center) tried so hard to please Puff that the stress got the better of him and he turned to drugs.

People in the music community were stunned by Puff's unprovoked attack on Shakir Stewart at LA Reid's wedding.

Enjoying a light moment at an after party with Pharell and a Bad Boy employee during a tour featuring Jay-Z and the Bad Boy Family.

A candlelight vigil near the nightclub where Anthony "Wolf" Jones (inset, right) and Lamont "Riz" Girdy (inset, left) were killed in 2003.

– Sandra Rose

When asked about allegations in this book, Puff told reporters
that he never produced my album because I only wrote two songs
for Bad Boy. But the credits on these Bad Boy releases – including
Puff's own albums – expose his response as yet another lie.

My parents, Lillie and Elma Kenneth Curry, were my Rock of Gibraltar through a decade of deception by Puff.

Mark Curry news

Diddy was in radio talking about the upcoming release from Curry. Mark Curry is in the studio as we speak and his selftitled album will hit the stores in summer of 2006.. You can hear Mark Curry with B5 in their bonus track titled "Friends".

After *XXL* and other hip hop magazines inquired about the release of my album, Puff told radio listeners in 2005 that he was releasing it in the summer of 2006. Our emails expose that as a lie.

From: IAMMC@aol.com
Date: Fri, 11 Feb 2005 02:55:29
To:badboy@tmo.blackberry.net
Subject: CURRY

Since i seems like we won't be putting that Mark Curry project out.. i feel i should be able to let you know something without feeling getting caught up. When i met you through Mac i was trying to become what i had to be. Good God blessed me with talent to tell the world about something real. Put yourself in my shoe and see if you can feel how i feel about it. Did you think i was playing with my life or something?

God Bless.
P.Diddy

U need to grow up then.
But if it makes u feel better to blame me then
feel better. All I did was give u a chance. I'm sorry
it didn't work out.

CHAPTER 17

Robbed

Just Mase and I struck up a friendship during the "No Way Out," tour, Black Rob and I also became close brothers at that time. Born in Spanish Harlem to an unwed mother, Robert "Black Rob" Ross had a troubled childhood.

He ran away from home in junior high and began committing felonies in order to survive. After several arrests, he spent most of his teen years living in group homes, juvenile detention centers, and jail.

Once he signed with Bad Boy in 1995, he thought that hard times were history. "When Puff came across me, it was in a time in my life when I was just doing a lot of wrong things," he states on his current web site. "For him to give me that hand and let me do what I do was a blessing. I just needed a chance."

Like most of us, Rob was under the impression that his first album would be released within a year. Instead, he spent the first year trying to write hits for Puff while trying to write something for himself at the same time.

Although Puff would offer a contract to any rapper whom he thought Russell Simmons planned to sign, he was too consumed with promoting Biggie to develop the talent once he paid for it. His refusal to delegate meant that Bad Boy could only handle one star at a time.

After Biggie's death, for instance, the only rapper getting Puff's attention was Mase. It was only after Mase told Puff that he was abandoning music that Puff finally gave Rob a chance. By then, Rob had grown disillusioned with Puff.

In August 1998 I was in the studio working with him on songs for his debut album, "Life Story." Harve Pierre was in charge of the project. He told me and Rob to listen to an instrumental to see what lyrical ideas we could come up with. I recited a verse to Harve which was similar to the one Rob wrote at the same time, but we all agreed that mine was more powerful. I went into the booth to record it.

"That's hot!" Harve shouted as I finished recording. "If Puff likes it, we'll record it that way." Puff loved it, so the song became "Muscle Game," or song Number 12 on "Life Story."

Rob and I immediately recognized that we worked well together, and so did others in the studio. I was more than happy when he asked me to do another song with him. The second number, "Down the Line," is the sixth song on the album.

Rob was happy that Puff was finally giving him his due, but he was also aware that Puff was only doing it out of desperation. He said that Puff never really believed in him.

When he told me how he planned to get back at Puff, it confirmed my sense that Puff had turned another friend into an enemy.

Rob formed the "Alumni," a rap group made up of myself, him, and two of his close friends who were rappers: Harlem-born G-Dep and southern-born rapper Petey Pablo. Prior to coming to Bad Boy, Rob was close to and often appeared in clubs with both of them. (Pablo moved to Harlem after making a name for himself in the South). All of us worked with him on the album.

One of the songs included a skit aimed at Puff. In the skit, a character named Shack Back asks:

"Yeah, you thought we couldn't do it, huh?" Shack then castigates his boss for doubting his skills, and even calls him a "freaky Friday ass nigga!"

When the album was finished, Puff refused to release it because he didn't think Black Rob was going to sell. Asked about the delay, Puff said that it was for Rob's own good, that his legal troubles would have hurt album sales if it was released according to schedule. Rob, Harve, me, and everyone else knew that was crap because the arrest of an artist almost always increased sales.

When Puff was finally forced to release Rob's album due to financial pressure, "Life Story" sold triple platinum. One of the songs on the album, "Whoa," is considered a classic.

The thing I remember most about Rob's success is how generous he was financially with those of us who helped him make the album. He also was able to persuade Puff to listen to some underground hits by G. Dep, one of his friends from back on the block.

Unfortunately, Rob spoke the truth to power after his album took off. He told fans and reporters in no uncertain terms that he was responsible for restoring Bad Boy's reputation as a place where new ground was being broken in hip hop. The comments irked Puff, who quietly started looking for someone to replace Rob.

Initially, I thought that it would be me. Music critics around the country were praising my skills, so I assumed that Puff would try to release my album before the buzz died. Instead, he turned to another artist that he had signed and that he treated like a lap dog: Shyne.

Some people might take offense about the comparison, so let me illustrate what I mean.

In the late 1990s, everyone in the jet-set crowd wanted to own an expensive pure-bred dog. Among the most popular at the time was the

Shar-Pei. Puff bought a Shar-Pei that he only fed the finest cuts of meat, bottled water, the whole nine yards. He named the dog "Honey" Combs, a wordplay on the cereal and his surname.

One day my friend Stef came to visit me while I was living in Puff's apartment. We went to Puff's place and Puff was bragging about how much money he paid for her and how much he spent feeding and grooming her. Stef was very knowledgeable about certain breeds, so he decided to play a trick on Puff to muzzle his non-stop bragging.

"I hate to tell you this, Puff," Stef said, "but your dog is not a pure-bred. It's mixed with something else." Stef then pointed out several aspects of the dog that indicated that it was a mutt.

Puff, who had been caressing the dog and carrying on until that moment, had a sudden change in behavior towards the dog that he probably wasn't even aware of. He played with the dog less and less. He kept glancing at the dog as it walked back and forth past us as if he was honing in on the features revealing its lack of pedigree.

A few months after that, Honey Combs was no longer a member of Puff's household. I was told that he shipped the dog down South somewhere because all of a sudden it didn't "have enough class" or pedigree to be seen with him. So when I say that Puff treated someone like a dog, remember Honey Combs.

Biggie's record sales shot through the stratosphere after his death. As a result, every hip hop label in the country was looking to sign any artist who sounded like him. On the East Coast, word on the street was that this young cat called Shyne had a voice that fit the bill.

Born in 1978 on the small island of Belize in Central America, Jamal "Shyne" Barrow was the son of a politician who in 2008 became prime minister of the nation. His father, however, rejected him soon after his birth, claiming that he was illegitimate. As a result, Barrow's mother fled the island and settled in Brooklyn.

Shyne fell under the influence of friends who soon had him selling drugs and wrapped up in gang warfare. He ended up getting shot in the arm during one showdown. Upon discovering that he had skills as a rapper, Shyne started focusing on a career in music.

In late 1997, the 19-year-old's reputation gained him an audition before Tommy Mottola of Sony, Jimmy Iovine of Interscope, Sylvia Rhone of Elektra, Russell Simmons and finally Puff. Once Puff realized that the rumors were true about Shyne sounding like Biggie, no amount of money in the world could have kept them apart.

Puff began courting Shyne days before the bidding. He showed up at Shyne's home in his freshly imported blue Bentley and gave him a top-of-the-line Rolex. During a bidding war, Puff ran away from the pack by bidding a million dollars. It was the highest signing fee in the history of hip hop at the time.

Puff had used a similar tactic to snare G-Dep within weeks of the Shyne deal. Trevell "G-Dep" Coleman was a functionally literate kid living in a Harlem housing project when Puff pulled up in the same Bentley used to snare Shyne. After luring G-Dep to his offices, Puff offered what seemed to him to be an offer he couldn't refuse: a $350,000 advance for a five-album deal.

Without offering the youngster any financial counseling or any constructive advice, Puff had him sign on the dotted line. Once the ink was dry, G-Dep started spending money like it grew on trees. After he spent nearly one-sixth of the advance, he discovered that taxes, production contracts, and stipulations held up the rest of his money. In less than six months, the kid was broke and in debt to Puff. He lost himself in a cesspool of drugs.

Puff had too much money invested in Shyne to let him befall a similar fate. He started hinting that he needed someone to mentor the youngster. So he asked me if it would be okay if Shyne moved into the apartment with me. It was his place, so what the hell was I supposed to say?

A few days later, Shyne moved into the smallest of the three bedrooms of the apartment. His room was in the rear and mine was in the front. The largest bedroom was in the center of the apartment and usually reserved for Puff. However, D-Mack would use it as a crash pad when he was in town.

Puff kept giving Shyne mixed signals. In private, he treated Shyne like was his son or little brother. But in public, he would be very critical and harsh. During an interview with *Newsweek,* for example, Puff dropped by the studio while Shyne was working on a new number. After calling Shyne over to demonstrate how much he sounded like Biggie, Puff felt like his newest star had let him down in front of the big shot reporter.

"You gotta stop writing rhymes without listening to the music first," he said as Shyne stood at attention. "You ain't riding the beat. That's the secret to why we not like these other cats. I need a star, not just a rapper."

The irony of Puff criticizing Shyne for sounding like those "other cats" is that he had personally ordered his next big star to study all of the early work of Snoop Dogg, NWA, and other so-called "gangster" rappers. He told Shyne to study their lyrics in order to understand why they struck such a responsive chord with black people. Essentially, he wanted Shyne to be a combination of Biggie and the Last Poets. That's a tall order any day.

Members of Junior M.A.F.I.A. saw Shyne as a poseur, so bad blood quickly developed between them. To escape the drama, Li'l Kim, the only female member of Junior M.A.F.I.A., began moving away from the group. Once she decided to go solo, Puff started dropping hints that they should get along with Shyne or seek another label.

Shyne walked around all day with music blaring from the headphones attached to the CD player. I'd watch him out of curiosity sometimes, lip synching to songs by NWA, Ghostface Killa and other gangster rappers.

One of the side effects of Puff's toughening up approach was that Shyne started to behave like a gangster. A few weeks after he moved in, I came home and found him sitting in the living room with an Ak47 rifle. The first thought that came to my mind is that the kid was about to do something stupid.

"Hey Mark," Shyne said as I entered the room, "I got a fuckin' bullet jammed in the chamber. Can you help me get it out?"

I probably could have, but there was no way that I wanted my fingerprints on that damn thing, so I pretended that I knew nothing about weapons.

"D-Mack will be here this evening," I replied. "He can probably fix that for you in a minute. He's good at that kind of stuff."

"Cool," he said. "This goddamn thing has been driving me crazy."

I didn't say anything to Puff about the incident. He was trying to make Shyne some kind of Manchurian Candidate anyway, so he would have been more amused than concerned about Shyne's mental state.

Days after the gun incident, Shyne came home around three o'clock in the morning with one of his buddies and two white girls. I could tell by the noise that they had been doing some serious drinking.

Shyne took one of the girls upstairs to his bedroom and turned on some music. Thirty minutes later, the second girl started talking loudly.

"Where is my friend?" she asked. "I'm ready to leave."

Shyne's buddy said something like he wasn't her friend's babysitter and that she should relax. He was trying to seduce her but it wasn't working. The young woman seemed to get more and more anxious.

She went upstairs and stood just outside the door and called her friend's name. "I'm ready to leave," she said. "Let's go."

Shyne's date came out of the room and the two of them left.

Someone started banging on the door an hour later. You know, when you're asleep in somebody else's house in the ghetto and someone starts banging on the door in the middle of the night, your first reaction is to lie perfectly still and hope that they go away. That's what I did, and apparently so did Shyne and his friend because the apartment was stone silent.

"Open the door!" the visitor demanded. "It's the police."

Hell, I wasn't sure if it was the police or not, so I didn't answer. You see that shit on TV all the time where some hitman dressed in a cop's uniform blows some jerk away after he answers a knock at the door.

I got out of bed and slowly crawled toward a window facing the street. It was two cops with the two white girls.

"Oh, shit!" I said to myself.

I remained quiet as the cop continued to knock.

141

"I know you're in there, Puff" he said, "so open the door."

He waited for about fifteen seconds, and then slid his card under the door.

"Here's my card," he said. "You'd better contact me right away."

After they left, I picked up the card. Shyne and his buddy came downstairs and asked whether the cops were gone.

"Yeah," I replied, "but them white girls were with 'em. There's gonna be trouble."

Puff called the house around seven o'clock.

"What the fuck's going on over there?" I got the cops calling my lawyer telling them that I've been accused of raping somebody."

You know the old saying about all black people looking alike. The tipsy women were under the impression that Shyne's buddy was Puff. So either the dude pretended to be Puff, the women had no idea what Puff looked like, or they were trying the lay the groundwork for a major lawsuit against a celebrity. Either way, the matter was dropped after police confirmed that Puff was nowhere near the apartment that night and that the women had not been molested in any way, shape or form.

At the same time that Shyne was confused about what Puff wanted him to be, he was confused about his own self-image. He started coming to the studio with five watches on and weird stuff like that. He would come to the studio under the influence, lay down some rhymes and then try to get everyone to agree that it was the most visionary thing ever written. It was only after he sobered up that he realized that it wasn't very good.

Shyne's demeanor changed after being around Puff for only a few months. I suppose that when somebody gives you the kind of money that Puff had given Shyne, it's difficult to remain humble. Having seen how Puff seemed to defy the law, Shyne started behaving like he was "Puff Jr."

142

CHAPTER 18

Like It's 1999

One morning Shyne asked me to go with him to a local car dealership. He had just received his money for signing his deal with Bad Boy and was ready to start buying a few dreams. The first thing on his list was a brand new 2000 Mercedes 600sl.

To my surprise, he approached the salesman with a cocky, even angry attitude. When he told the dealer all of the features that he wanted on the car, the salesman replied that it had to be ordered.

"I want the car now," Shyne answered, "or I'll buy it somewhere else."

The salesman explained again that no one would have the car in stock that he wanted because he wanted too many extras. After I talked to him, he started to calm down. Once he accepted the dealer's word, he settled for a car they had in stock, which was still a 600sl. He paid six figures for it.

Shyne took delivery of the car the next day. I could tell immediately that he didn't know how to drive very well by the way he drove off of the lot. He had probably just gotten his license. He headed straight for the studio to show the car to Puff.

"Man," Puff said in disappointment, "I have millions of dollars and I don't even have a car that cost that much."

A few days later, Shyne came home with the passenger-side rearview mirror missing. When I asked what happened, he told me that he sideswiped a parked car. A week later, he came back with one of the windows shot out. When I asked what happened, he told me that he was over a young lady's house when her boyfriend came home and started shooting.

A few nights after that, I received a call from the hospital and was told that Shyne was involved in a car accident. It turned out that he had picked up his cousin and two childhood friends for a night of partying. Police said that Shyne was apparently speeding and suddenly found himself on the tail of another car.

He lost control and the Mercedes ran off the road. By the time police arrived, one of Shyne's friends was already dead. Part of the rear axle had penetrated his back, causing fatal injuries. Everyone but Shyne was seriously injured.

When I walked into the hospital, Shyne was in bed. I told the doctor that I was an immediate family member, so they let me see him. The doctor cautioned me not to tell him about the fatality because they didn't want him to go into shock.

The courts revoked Shyne's New York driver's license after the accident, but he still had a Florida license. He seemed to walk around in a daze for weeks after learning of his friend's death, but rumors to the contrary were in the streets. One rumor had him talking and laughing at the friend's funeral, and another had it that he only offered to pay a small portion of the funeral expenses.

Since I was supposed to be keeping an eye on Shyne, I felt a tinge of guilt. But I had warned Puff that something bad was going to happen in that car because it was too much for Shyne and the kid was getting high all the time. Unfortunately, Puff had his hands full with his own personal problems.

A few weeks after Kim Porter gave birth in 1997, Puff started sneaking around with Jennifer Lopez, a mediocre dancer who had gained fame in the early 1990s as one of the few Latino women on the hit TV show, "In Living Color." When the show ended in 1994, she won major roles in several films, including the lead role in a movie based on the life and murder of Selena Quintanilla-Pérez. Despite her marginal vocal talent, Lopez had dreams of becoming a recording superstar. Puff met Lopez through Benny Medina, who served as a manager of sorts for both of them.

She made cameos on several singles produced by Puff after they started dating. By the end of 1998, however, they were working on her debut album. During that time, Kim would contact me when she couldn't find him. Puff would have me lie to her. It typically involved telling her that he was at the studio recording and couldn't be reached, in a business meeting, or something along those lines.

In exchange for the lies, or maybe just to avoid too many questions from the gossip magazines, Puff would frequently have me tag along on their dates. On one occasion, we were hanging out in Florida when a photographer snapped a photo of the three of us riding motorbikes.

When the picture got prominent play in *People* magazine, Kim knew that Puff had been lying about the nature of his relationship with Lopez. At first Puff seemed to fear what would happen if Kim found out. But once he and Lopez started talking about marriage, he took on a devil-may-care attitude. That was his frame of mind in December 1999.

By then, Shyne had fully recovered physically from the car accident, but it seems like part of his soul died. Puff was no doubt trying to salvage his investment in Shyne, so he started keeping close tabs on him. The two were nearly inseparable.

Shyne had already demonstrated his loyalty to Puff, most notably during the attack in August 1999 on Rev. Roger Mills. Of all those who battered him outside the radio station, Mills distinctly recalled Shyne being overly aggressive.

His strident defense let Puff know that Shyne was willing to lay down his life for Puff. Two days after Christmas 1999, he did.

Getting a jump on the New Year's celebration, Puff decided to go club-hopping in New York. Wardel Fenderson, Puff's personal week-end chauffeur, arrived at the studio at eleven o'clock and picked up Puff, Lopez, and Shyne in a new silver Lincoln Navigator owned by Bad Boy Entertainment. He dropped them off a few minutes later near a popular night spot in Manhattan.

As they exited the car, Puff told Fenderson to wait outside the club until he received a call from "Curtis Jones," a cheesy code for Anthony "Wolf" Jones, of course.

Wolf leaned against a limousine as the trio walked a few yards to Club New York. The club's owner recalled that about 30 people entered the club with Puff's entourage, most of them groupies.

When a security staffer told Puff and his crew to pass through the metal detector, Wolf approached him and whispered in his ear that he should let them through without a search. The guard complied and another guard led them to the VIP section.

Shyne had a .9mm Ruger stuck in his waistband. Whether Puff was armed as well would become a bone of contention. Suffice it to say that either Puff or Wolf was carrying a .40-caliber handgun that had been stolen in Atlanta four months earlier.

As they left the club, Puff expected the crowd to part for him the way the Red Sea did for Moses. The problem was some of the party-goers were there to party and not to star-gaze. To fix this lack of attention, Puff, who had about $10,000 in his pocket, started tossing hundred dollar bills into the air.

A few people started diving for them, but most people were insulted. The eager beavers started bumping and pushing others to get the money. Matthew Allen, who was sitting at the bar, was pushed forward by someone, forcing his face to nearly hit the bar. As he was pushed, his turned his head, knocking over his drink.

As Puff headed toward the exit, a group of party-goers approached him and told him that what he had done was pretty foul. To illustrate, a man who was accidentally struck by the people scrambling for the money pulled a wad of bills out of his pocket and started tossing them over the heads of Puff and Lopez.

According to witnesses, Puff and Shyne both drew weapons and started shooting. Nearly everyone in the club was shocked by the gunfire because they thought that the metal detectors prevented armed patrons from getting into the club.

At least three patrons were injured by gunfire in the melee. Puff, Lopez and Wolf dashed from the club and jumped into the Navigator.

"Go, go, go, go, go!" they yelled as Fenderson sped off.

Police arrived on the scene just as Shyne was coming out and nabbed him. After he surrendered, they retrieved the gun tucked under his belt.

Wolf and Puff ordered Fenderson to drive as fast as he could and not to stop for anyone or anything. Knowing of Wolf's reputation for hurting people and getting away with it, Fenderson did what he was told. As the car sped down the street, a witness testified that he saw the hand of a brown person toss a handgun out of the car's window.

With police in hot pursuit, the chauffeur ran through a dozen red lights. When the Navigator was confronted with a police roadblock, Wolf grabbed the steering wheel and yelled at Fenderson to keep going.

Fenderson saw a gun tucked under Puff's belt as the mogul stood up and tried to get rid of it. Puff and Wolf were trying to stash the gun in a secret compartment in the Navigator but they didn't know the trick to opening it.

The roadblock turned out to be the end of the line. As the cops approached the vehicle, one of them peered through the window and saw Puff sitting next to Lopez. Puff was leaning forward toward Wolf's seat with his hands between his legs. He yelled at Puff to put his hands in the air several times before Puff complied. When they opened the doors, police found a handgun on the floor under the rear of Wolf's seat and in front of Puff's feet.

Puff started setting up his escape hatch as soon as he was arrested. He asked the officer driving the car why all four of them were being arrested. The officer said that they were all arrested because no one would admit to possession of the gun found under Wolf's seat.

"What would happen if someone admitted to having the gun?" Puff asked.

The officer said they'd have to see what would happen once they arrived at the precinct.

"Okay, deal," Puff replied. "When we get back to the precinct I'll tell you whose gun it is".

During the personal inventory search, police removed over $8,000 from Puff's pocket, including 81 one-hundred dollar bills. This partially substantiated statements by patrons that he was throwing hundred dollar bills into the air.

As the three of them stood before the desk sergeant to fill out paperwork, Puff began offering bribes to Wolf and Fenderson. The sergeant watched as Puff whispered something in Wolf's ear and Wolf shook his head from side to side.

Using coded words, Wolf told Puff that he would be convicted under the new habitual offender laws if he took the rap, and would go back to prison for decades because he was already on probation.

Then Puff started whispering something into Fenderson's ear.

"I'll give you fifty thousand dollars and this pinkie ring if you say the gun is yours," he said. When it seemed that Puff was badgering the chauffeur, the sergeant intervened and told them to quiet down.

Sensing what was going on, police placed Puff and Fenderson in the same holding cell. Sure enough, Fenderson called out to one of the officers a couple of hours later and said: "The gun was mine."

But a few more hours later, Fenderson realized the implications of what he was agreeing to after he learned that people in the club had been injured by gunfire. He contacted the same office and frantically recanted his confession.

"That gun wasn't mine," he said. "I was lying. . . I'm not taking the rap for anybody!"

Puff was shaken up by the chauffeur's change of heart.

His offer to Fenderson was just the beginning. After posting bail that morning, Puff and Wolf went into high gear contacting potential witnesses against them. On December 30, Puff called the chauffeur to make a mysterious offer, one that prosecutors interpreted as another attempted bribe. Fearing that he was being set up, Fenderson taped the call as his boss said:

> "I was just thinking about you, Dog. I know you're probably going through a lot of shit . . . I'm calling to let you know that I'm there for you . . . I'm just concerned. That news you hit me with earlier really fucked me up and I just wanna make you feel like comfortable, you know what I'm saying? Make your family feel comfortable and let you know that everything gonna be alright. . ."

A day or so later, Puff contacted Allen, the man at the bar who said that he saw Puff brandishing a gun, and promised to give him money if he kept his mouth shut.

"I've already got a bribery on me," Puff told Allen. "My boys will take care of you but you got to understand that it's not coming from me. Give your number to my man, Wolf."

Puff retained Johnnie Cochran and a prominent New York law firm to represent him. Any good attorney coaches his client before trial, but it seems that what Puff said before the grand jury went well beyond coaching.

Just as he had done when the nine kids were trampled to death in 1991, Puff put his hand on the Holy Bible and swore to tell the whole truth and nothing but the truth to the grand jury investigating the crimes.

"I am telling you [that] I swear to God on my children, I am telling you the God honest truth from my heart . . . I would never have gotten in the Navigator if I knew there was a gun in that car. I did not come to the club in that car. I came to the club in a limousine and I planned to leave in the limousine."

In fact, from the moment he took the stand until the moment he stepped down, he told some of the worst lies that anyone has ever heard.

"The only person I saw and I knew [who] came in with me was Anthony Jones," Puff claimed. "I did not know that Shyne was going to be there, and I did not see any actions that he did. . . I am one hundred percent innocent. . . I never offered nobody any money to do anything wrong."

Not only did he seem to deny that he arrived at the club with Shyne, but with Lopez as well. He accused Fenderson of lying because the chauffeur was after his money. Yet he offered no logical reason about how Fenderson could drive the Navigator and wipe off fingerprints from the gun at the same time, and then place the gun under the rear of Wolf's seat.

The prosecutor had reason to believe that Puff was giving perjured testimony, so he let him keep talking.

Puff brought up the Steve Stoute incident. When asked why he assaulted and battered Stoute, Puff released another batch of pure, unadulterated lies.

"I had a fistfight with a man called Stephen Stoute and I admitted to it one hundred percent."

Asked if he and two other men attacked Stoute with a bottle, a chair, and a telephone, Puff reacted as though he was insulted.

"That is not true, Sir," he began. "I got into a physical fight. I did not touch him with a bottle. I did not have any help [from] anybody else."

He also claimed that he was only accompanied by Paul "Ox" Oxford to Stoute's office, and that they bumped into one of Ox's friends "that just happened to be there. I do not know his exact name."

When I heard about Puff's grand jury testimony, I thought about the early morning phone call from D-Mack telling me that he was sitting next to Puff, who wanted to sign me to Bad Boy. I thought about all the times that D-Mack had slept in Puff's apartment after I moved in.

Since Puff had known D-Mack's real name for years, it was a clear that his swear upon his children was bedeviled. There were dozens of contracts proving that Puff knew exactly what D-Mack's real name was, and there were dozens of photos of them together. I know because I'm in some of those photos.

CHAPTER 19

Shoo, Shyne

An old trick in criminal cases is for the defense to delay the trial for as long as possible. Witnesses move on or become forgetful or key facts, evidence get misplaced or contaminated, and victims have to file personal injury lawsuits. When a person is injured during a crime, they have to file a civil lawsuit within a very short time frame or else lose the right to do so. The period is sometimes only a year.

In delaying the criminal trial, defense attorneys put the injured witness in a bind. If he doesn't file a lawsuit before the criminal trial starts a year or so later, the injured witness may run out of time for filing a personal injury action. But if they file a lawsuit before the trial ends, defense lawyers will try to convince the jury that the witness is lying on the defendant in criminal court in order to win money later in the civil court.

That was the case here. Although Puff, Wolf and Shyne were arrested in December 1999, the trial didn't start until January 2001. The Court denied a request by Wolf and Shyne for separate trials, thereby creating a crabs-in-a-barrel situation. Shyne ended up using two lawyers that he met through Puff, a decision his mother would later raise serious questions about.

In the end, Puff was able to pull himself out of the barrel by crawling over his codefendants, witnesses, and the truth.

Ballistics tests clearly demonstrated that one bullet hole in the ceiling was exactly where it should have been if Puff had fired a gun while standing where witnesses claimed.

The most damaging testimony came from Puff's weekday chauffeur, Bill Williamson. He said that he was not working that Friday night, but that Puff had specifically requested that the night's chauffeur pick him up in the silver Navigator. Puff's lawyers called a chauffeur who claimed that he had driven Lopez and Puff to the club that night in a black limousine.

Williamson also said that neither Puff nor Wolf knew how to open the new car's secret compartment. That would explain why the policemen saw Puff frantically fumbling with something while leaning over behind Wolf's seat and why Puff tried to bribe Fenderson.

When the jury first began deliberations, eight of the dozen favored convicting Puff on at least one charge. However, name-calling erupted in the jury room, with some black jurors accusing white jurors of being racists. One evoked the controversial Amadou Diallo case to compare what was happening to Puff.

Once they split up along racial lines, an acquittal was all but assured. More petty arguments developed, with several jurors saying that they didn't believe the witnesses against Puff because many of them had filed million dollar personal injury suits against him and thus had a motive to lie. The old ploy had worked once again.

Reporters noted on several occasions that many of the female jurors were repeatedly making eye contact with Puff and smiling at him. A star-struck jury rarely lets the truth get in the way, and that's probably another reason why Puff walked.

When Puff took the stand, he basically told the same story that he had rehearsed for the grand jury. To believe Puff's testimony, you would have to believe that all of the witnesses who saw him holding a gun were liars, that Steve Stoute lied about being assaulted, that his personal chauffeur Fenderson lied about picking him up that night and lied about Puff trying to bribe him, that Matthew Allen lied about Puff trying to bribe him, that police lied about a gun found near the club and in the Navigator and about Puff trying to bribe Wolf and Fenderson at the station, and that all those phone logs showing calls from Wolf or Puff to witnesses were merely coincidental.

In reflecting on the case, Ron Kuby, the renowned criminal defense lawyer, said that Puff is either "the unluckiest person in the world, being bedeviled by a string of bad coincidences, or he's guilty."

In March 2001 – fifteen months after the ordeal began – a jury inexplicably acquitted Puff and Wolf, but found Shyne guilty. The prosecutor was outraged. He essentially accused Puff of giving perjured testimony, not only during the trial but also before the grand jury.

"What does that tell you about his own consciousness of guilt?" he asked the jury during his closing argument. "The fact that he lied so brazenly before the grand jury and before you because he knows he's guilty."

Puff, he concluded "is an egregious liar."

When Puff was trying to get Shyne to sign with Bad Boy, Shyne's mother said that she would approve on the condition that Puff exercise parental and custodial supervision over him since Shyne was still a minor. Puff promised to be a good daddy to her boy.

But on the witness stand, Puff denied that Shyne was his special charge. "The personal relationship I have with all my artists is about the same," he said.

Everybody at Bad Boy knew that was a lie. It made the staff wonder whether anything Puff said under oath was true. His false testimony and the testimony of a key witness left Shyne's mother in nearly a state of shock.

A witness who told police that Puff was armed that night turned around and testified that she never saw him with a gun. She said that Shyne was the only person she saw with a gun that night.

After the woman finished giving her new version of events, Puff walked over to Shyne's mother and made an odd statement: "I'm sorry. I'm sorry."

"She totally changed her story," his mother said in disbelief.

Shyne was convicted because he refused to tell the jury the truth about what Puff did that night, because he didn't want to be known as a snitch, and because he believed that Puff cared about him. He would take "death before dishonor," he said. It was only after the trial ended that Shyne realized that Puff didn't give a damn about him or anyone else.

"As soon as we were indicted," Shyne told the *Village Voice* after the trial, "he wanted me to keep away from him. He didn't even want to put my album out. Throughout the trial, it was like, "You get outta this however you can and I'm gonna get outta this however I can."

Shyne didn't help his cause during the trial by getting into another bad car accident. When the media reported that he was driving without a license at the time, it painted a negative image in the mind of New Yorkers, and it may have been as damaging as the court testimony against him.

Nation of Islam Minister Conrad Muhammad was among those who criticized Puff for his mistreatment and betrayal of Shyne.

"Shyne's mother and grandmother placed this young man in the care and custody of Sean "Puffy" Combs, who they believed was a responsible executive of a company," Muhammad said.

"Puffy has the same responsibility as a teacher, as a coach. This boy, Shyne, was out with his idol on that fateful night. When I put my child in your hands, I don't expect him to end up dead or in jail."

Shyne cried as the verdict against him was read. Puff, by contrast, sat next to his lawyers staring at the Holy Bible like a divinity student.

After being acquitted, Puff went before the cameras once again and started thanking God for essentially helping him escape justice. He was going to learn from the incident, he vowed, and return to being the choirboy he once was. It was vintage bullshit from a vintage bullshitter.

If we are to learn anything from Johnnie Cochran's defense of O.J. Simpson and Puff, it is that a high-priced lawyer is like a high-priced call girl: he will say and do anything if the price is right.

As Puff was taken away from the courthouse in a limousine, Shyne was taken to a holding cell. On June 1, he stood before the judge and made a final plea for justice and compassion.

"I never meant to hurt nobody," the 21-year-old said in a trembling voice. He begged the judge to be merciful and "not to waste my life."

While praising Shyne's talent, the judge gave him a harsh sentence. Shyne would have to serve a minimum of eight and one-half years before he would be eligible for parole.

Puff had once again escaped justice, and once again people who believed in him were paying for it. Shyne sacrificed his music career and freedom for Puff. Now the man who financed Puff's record label was about to be stripped of his own label due to Puff's erratic behavior and criminal activity.

Days after the Club New York incident, BMG decided that Puff had become too much of a liability. Since Clive Davis had already been admonished after the Stoute incident, BMG wasted no time putting plans in motion to fire him.

BMG officials quietly offered Davis' job to LA Reid, and purchased Atlanta-based LaFace Records for $100 million in exchange for Reid accepting the job. Once Reid accepted, Davis was given his walking papers.

Reid was the person who brought Puff to Davis for seed money after Harrell fired Puff over the trampling deaths. Davis not only gave him the money, but also gave him the studio that became "Daddy's

House." Reid had remained close to Puff ever since then, and was in fact a partner in Justin's, the Atlanta restaurant named for Puff's son. Reid was Justin's godfather.

In June 2000 while awaiting trial, Puff flew to the island of Capri in Italy to attend Reid's marriage to schoolteacher Erica Holton. Guests were assigned to either the Palace Hotel or the Caesar Augustus.

By then, Lopez was already distancing herself from Puff. Her family, managers, and friends warned her to avoid him, and fans actually started petitions asking her to distance herself from Puff before the relationship ruined her career. Once he finally accepted that Lopez was gone, he immediately began courting Kim Porter once more.

The only problem was that Kim had put their relationship in the past. She was seeing Shakir Stewart, head of Atlanta-based Hitco Music Publishing. Reid had just made Shakir a consultant to LaFace.

Puff ran into Kim on the island. Somehow he found out about a phone message from Shakir to Kim.

"How are my babies doing?" Shakir asked her.

When Puff realized that Kim was doing fine without him, he was ready to kill. After summoning a couple of his bodyguards, Puff left the Palace and went to Shakir's room at the other hotel. He bammed on Shakir's door until he answered it.

"What the fuck you doing leaving messages on my bitch's cell phone?" Puff raged. "Where you get off saying you the daddy of my kids?"

Shakir knew that Puff never confronted anyone without backup, so he was afraid to defend himself.

He tried to explain to Puff that he and Kim were only friends and that he was joking around when he left the message. But he also told Puff that he had no business trying to run the life of a woman that he had repeatedly abandoned.

Puff called him a liar and some other expletives, then picked up a chair and clobbered Shakir with it. As Shakir crumpled to the floor, Puff ran away from the hotel with his guards and returned to his hotel.

Reid was furious when he discovered how Puff had attacked Shakir, and at his wedding, no less. He knew that Puff was under a lot of pressure from the pending trial, but nothing justified his attack. The incident became a turning point in their friendship. Reid finally understood why Benny Medina had concluded that Puff was out of control and incorrigible.

Although Shakir tried to keep word of the beating from traveling, everyone at the wedding soon knew about it, and by the time he returned to Atlanta, someone had leaked it to the media.

"This is a stupid and ridiculous rumor which is absolutely one hundred percent not true," Puff said through a spokesman. It was a carbon copy of his denial in the Stoute incident.

Shakir was so afraid of Puff's henchmen coming to his offices in Atlanta to finish him off that he avoided going to work for weeks. He also refused all requests to discuss the attack with the media. Those of us who knew him felt bad because Shakir was a good brother, and a businessman who tried to do right by his artists. Just ask Beyonce Knowles, one of the first artist he signed to Hitco, and singer Ciara, whom he signed days after taking on duties at LaFace.

They say that some people use God like a spare tire; they only seek Him when they get a flat. They become prayerful and worship that tire until it gets them where they're going. But once they put a new tire on that car, they toss the spare back into a well in the trunk and forget all about how it saved them on a dark road one rainy night.

Music was the last thing on Puff's mind after he was charged in the club shooting. He was praying and holding that cross around neck every chance he got. He was less arrogant but more cranky.

He developed a severe case of ulcers but was so stressed out that he ignored the doctor's orders to stay away from liquor. The public probably didn't notice it, but he lost a lot of weight in a short period because he would lose his appetite for days at a time.

Once the ordeal was over, Puff forgot about all those promises he made about becoming a better man. He forgot about that promise that he and Johnnie Cochran made to try to help out Shyne. It didn't matter to Shyne, though, because he had already denounced Puff as a Judas. He asked to be released from his contract with Bad Boy and was quickly offered a new multimillion dollar deal with Def Jam.

While he was preparing for the trial, nothing was getting done at Bad Boy. BMG and fans everywhere had been holding their breath in anticipation of the release of Shyne's debut album, but that was the first thing that was put on hold.

The news media went haywire with announcements about the death of Bad Boy and the end of Puff's career. The death of Bad Boy was great exaggerated but the company really was in dire straits. Puff had paid so much money in legal fees that he had to fire nearly half of Bad Boy's staff to balance the budget.

Since there was nothing for me to do in New York during the hiatus, I packed my things and moved back to Atlanta. Deirdre gave birth to our first child on April 1, 2001. We named him Mark Curry II. He was born on the same day as his grandfather. The morning he was born, his grandfather died.

Faith Evans and her husband Todd where living in Atlanta at that time. I was out and about one day when I ran into Todd. He asked me whether I planned to go to Miami to work with Puff on his new album.

"Faith is gonna be there working on hers," he said. "They're gonna call it Faithfully."

Within days of the encounter, I started getting calls from friends and associates asking me the same question.

It turned out that Puff had flown to Miami shortly after being acquitted and was working on a new album which he planned to call "The Saga Continues." When I heard that, all I could say was: "Ain't that a bitch."

The reason was very obvious why I didn't know about it. I had warned Puff many times to take care of Shyne the way he promised his family that he would. Having me around him would have forced Puff to face some ugly truths about his mistreatment of Shyne. So I supposed he was ready to forget about me the same way that he had forgotten about Shyne.

As my son slept on my chest one night, I found it so soothing that I quickly fell asleep myself. But as I slept, an inner voice kept telling me to go to Miami. I always listen to my inner voice.

Shoo, Shyne

I called my friend Stef in the middle of the night and asked him if he could get two buddy passes and come with me to Miami. I told him the details of what was happening. He agreed that I should follow my instincts, but said that he was unable to go due to scheduling problems.

I went to his house the next morning and picked up the buddy pass for American Airlines. With Mase, Black Rob and Shyne gone, we talked hopefully about Puff finally having enough vision to start on my album.

While we were talking, my wife called and told me to bring home some Similac and a few groceries. Since my flight was leaving in a few hours, Stef agreed to drop me off at the airport. He parked next to me on the supermarket's lot and I rushed inside to grab a few things.

My mine was racing a mile a minute as I walked down the aisles of the store. One minute I was talking to a friend in Miami, trying to get him to pick me up from the airport when I got there. He told me that his friend, who was also one of my fans, would pick me up. The next minute I was talking to my wife again because I had forgotten some of the items she wanted. Then I was talking to Bad Boy family members in New York to see about living arrangements.

I pulled out a batch of papers when I got to the counter, extracted a twenty and paid the cashier. As I walked back to the car, I reached into my pocket for the keys. It suddenly occurred to me that I had lost the buddy pass. I could have sworn it was in the same pocket as my keys. I checked and rechecked my pockets with no luck. I searched the car several times and still couldn't find it. The pass was gone.

CHAPTER 20

Bad Boys for Life

At first I took that as a sign for me not to go. No sooner had the thought crossed my mind that Stef rolled down his window and asked me what was wrong. I was too embarrassed to say it but I told him that I misplaced the pass.

"I knew it," he said, "because you got a look on your face like you're about to cry."

He got out of his car and approached me. He reached into his back pocket and pulled out another buddy pass. I got a little mad at first because I thought that he had played a mean trick on me.

"I got two passes yesterday," he said, "because I was seriously thinking about going with you. But since you lost yours, take mine. I'll come down later."

I shocked him and myself by giving him a hug because what he had done felt like a miracle. "The Lord works in mysterious ways," I said. I rushed home, gave Deirdre the groceries and goodbye kisses, and headed for the airport.

Mind you, I had no idea where Puff and the gang were staying in Miami. When I arrived at the airport, this guy known as Kinje picked me up. Since I was told that he was a fan I thought he would be a kid, but he was older than me. I didn't know where to go, but I knew where Puff liked to hang out in Miami, so I suggested going by South Beach.

As soon as we got on the strip in South Beach, I noticed Puff driving down the street in his Bentley. We pulled up on him at the light. D-Mack was in the car with him. He told me to follow them to the studio.

When I got there, nearly the whole Bad Boy roster was there. Even Loon, who helped us write the songs for the "Forever" album, was present. From the way he was acting, I knew that Puff was planning to make Loon his next big artist.

Puff went into the studio for a few minutes while I waited in the hall. After he came out, I asked him point blank why he hadn't invited me to Miami.

"Honestly, Mark, you just ain't got it no more," he said as he avoided looking into my face. "The only reason you're still part of the label is because my man Harve still believes in you."

Harve and I both looked at each other and laughed. We laughed because we both knew that Puff didn't know what he was talking about. At home and at Bad Boy, everyone knew that I was the one who first taught Puff how to rap. They knew that I had written in part or in whole many of his biggest hits.

Here was a man who had never written a complete song in his life telling me that my well of talent was dry. I probably would have punched him in the face if Harve and I hadn't been laughing so hard.

After he realized how ridiculous he sounded, he made me an offer.

"I have a track you can work on, alright?" he said. "If it don't sound like a hit, there's nothing else I can do for you and you need to go home because I'm on a tight budget."

Over the next couple of days, I noticed that Loon was by Puff's side every time I saw either of them. Clearly he was being groomed as Shyne's replacement, the new sensation readying for launch out of Bad Boy's cannon.

When I first arrived at the studio to begin work, most people were happy to see me, but a few people seemed upset that I was there. The happy ones were the ones who felt like I brought good luck to Puff's albums, and the unhappy ones were the ones who knew that another person would now be getting a part of their publishing pie.

So much was going on inside the crowded space that it was distracting. People were falling over themselves trying to please Puff, who had returned to his old narcissistic ways now that the trial was over and that he had quietly settled things with Shakir Stewart over the assault at LA Reid's wedding. I told the other writers that I was gonna go soak up some rays while working on the song.

Kinje drove me around Miami in his truck as we listened to music and I wrote lyrics. When we pulled back up to the studio several hours later, I knew that what I had written would be a hit.

Everybody came out to the truck to hear what I had come up with. When they heard it, they couldn't suppress their reaction. They were dancing around the truck and bobbing their heads. Puff was flabbergasted when he heard it. Harve and I teased him about the comments he made when I pulled up as an uninvited guest.

The song was titled "Bad Boy for Life." After we finished that one, I recorded several others, including "Blast Off," "Where's Sean," "Lonely," and "Last Song." I also wrote Puff's verses on "Ride With Me." You can hear all of those on "The Saga Continues."

Not everyone was happy about my productivity, of course. I was there for only three weeks but I produce more material for the album than anyone else.

Puff did almost no writing for the album because he was in the middle of luring in New Edition to Bad Boy. They were also in Miami preparing to work on their album. Bobby Brown had long ago left and a couple of more members had tried to strike out on their own with limited success. The minute their contract with MCA expired, Puff signed them to Bad Boy.

We flew to LA on July 2 to record the "Bad Boy for Life" video at Universal Theaters. People kept telling me that my part was the hottest of all and wanted to know when my album was being released. All I could say was that we'd have to see what happens once we got back to New York.

When we did the video, which runs six minutes, Puff delayed putting me in it until after the skit featuring actor Ben Stiller. That's roughly three minutes into the video. Consequently, my appearance in the video was hardly ever aired because the skit made the song too long for TV. Most stations stopped the video after the Puff-Stiller confrontation.

Also, if you watch the video on Youtube or other online video sites, you'll notice that when I do my verse he hardly gives the camera time to focus on me. Instead, he devotes my verse to cameos by Shaquille O'Neill, Mike Tyson, and himself.

The same is true for Black Rob's appearance. None of us who did the actual writing got more than twenty seconds of exclusive camera time. Puff got more than four minutes. That's how narcissistic he is. Suge Knight's words from 1994 still rang true.

When the video premiered on July 10, my family was really upset about how Puff was hogging the camera. We laughed as my brothers joked about wanting to "put a hurtin' on the boy," for being so self-absorbed. I told everyone to calm down because my day was coming, and that I was just happy to be in it and with Bad Boy.

For the next couple of months we stayed pretty busy. We went on David Letterman's show, "Soul Train" and others, and we appeared on the cover of the *Source Magazine* doing a "Men in Black" imitation.

On September 6th we did the MTV Music awards. Puff wanted to perform so badly for this event he was beside himself. We all met up at Puff's hotel to go to the awards. He wanted us to seem like a real family in the eyes of fans.

When I got to the hotel, they told me the plan. We were going to pull up to the red carpet performing "Bad Boy for Life" on a flat bed truck. We were running short on time and everybody was in a rush, so we had to improvise. I ended up wearing a medium-size outfit when I normally wear a triple extra-large. I felt uncomfortable at the awards how but once again, I was just happy to be there.

I thought about Puff's comments about my career being over as friends and fans called me or sent me news stories about the song. Some of the reviews were from as far away as Europe.

"The album is preceded by the single, "Bad Boy for Life," Gareth Thomas of *Music and Media* wrote in September 2001, "which sees P Diddy's distinctive style blending with Black Rob and Bad Boy rising star Mark Curry on the cut-up, raucous track."

While some reviewers didn't think much of the album, Black Rob and I were usually singled out for praise. "Bad Boy 4 Life" is another good track, featuring Black Rob and newcomers Mark Curry," reported Jamar Thrasher for an urban newswire. "Its old school beat and lyrics show that Combs knows what he's doing. . . The album is well rounded . . . but could have done without Diddy, an egotistical song all about Combs."

As a result of all the good publicity I received, Puff promised to release my album if I could produce one more song that he felt had hit potential. I flew to New York and checked into the hotel that he paid for out of my publishing and went to work.

When I stay at a hotel, I always sleep with the TV on but with the volume muted. Normally I wouldn't wake up until after noon, but I woke up shortly after nine o'clock one morning after I was there for three weeks. The loud sounds of emergency vehicle sirens bounced off the walls, so many sirens that it seemed like every fire truck, police car and ambulance was just outside the hotel. I had no view of the street from my room, so I had no idea of what was happening.

As I was watching the news with the sound still muted, it seemed to be showing fire from one of the World Trade Center towers. I was still groggy and assumed that the fire would be out soon and that the building had been evacuated. All of a sudden the ground shook and the lights in the Hotel started blinking.

As I continued to watch, an aircraft headed towards the other tower and slammed right into it.

"Oh, my God!" I said out loud. I opened the door and all you could see were people running toward the elevators and exits trying to get out of the building.

I decided to take a quick shower and hurry downtown to the studio to see if everyone was okay. The moment I got in, the hotel lost power and the water started getting cold. I got dressed and left.

When I walked outside, it felt like I was on a horror movie set. People were crying, yelling and screaming and running for cover. Everyone was covered with a grayish powder. I watched my feet as the powder covered my soles and then my whole shoe the closer I got to the studio. It took me thirty minutes to walk to the studio but I was so shocked by life around me that it seemed like five.

When I arrived at Daddy's House, the receptionist was packing her things up. She said that they where shutting the studio down because it was just a block away from Times Square and Times Square was believed to be a target, too.

Everybody was leaving the city to go home to be with his or her family. I wanted to go home to be with my family, too, but the airport was shut down. Not only that, they told me that I couldn't stay in the studio because I would be locked inside if the building lost power. I made my way back to hotel.

For the first time in probably a century, there were almost no cabs or crowded streets in downtown New York City. People left the city en masse on September 11, turning the Big Apple into a ghost town.

For the next week, it remained that way. I called home to let my family know that I was safe. Everyday I hoped that I would be able to get out of New York and get back home to Atlanta, but interstate transportation from the city was completely shut down. Everyday I walked up to the studio but nobody was ever there. I was literally stranded in

New York. Luckily, the hotel understood the situation and didn't complain about payment after my booking dates expired.

The attack brought out the patriotism of most Americans. As the country tried to return to normal, entertainers volunteered to give free concerts to take people's minds off fears of another attack. Puff ordered military fatigues for all of his artists and we toured the country with most of the biggest names in music, including Rod Stewart, Destiny's Child, and the Backstreet Boys.

By early 2002, Bad Boy returned to business as usual. We were added to the Britney Spears tour for a few spot dates because promoters wanted to test Puff's crossover appeal after the series of patriotic performances we did. Puff had added NSYNC's management to his team with intentions of cross-promoting. It was pure love the way crowds responded to us. When it came time for me to do my verses of our songs, I could hear fans singing it with me and that feeling gave me an extra charge.

In February 2002 "Bad Boy for Life" was nominated for a Grammy. I was on a Cloud Nine. It reminded me of when my song "Come With Me" was nominated for "Best Video from a Film." A month later we were added on to NYSNC's celebrity tour.

I was feeling good with the progress I was making. It felt like my career was finally taking off. I couldn't wait to talk to my father to share my good fortune. I was about to have the career that he had always wanted. I wanted him to see him dream come true through me.

I called his phone number but it had been disconnected. I called my grandmother's house in Clermont, Florida to see if she had heard from him.

"Yes, Mark," she said softly, "your daddy's here. He's real bad off, Baby. Real sick." I felt like I was going to faint as I asked her what was wrong with him.

"He's got cancer, Mark," she replied. "It's in the final stages so there's nothing that can be done for him."

Tears ran down my face as our times together flashed before me. Then I thought about how sad it was that he had to go home and let his mother take care of him. All of those women in his life, the ones that he thought would be by his side forever, were nowhere to be found.

My father had many children, but none of them had risen to the top of their profession. None of them were in such a distinguished place that they could afford to take care of Dad in his final years. When you look at your children and see that they've grown to be strong adults, you die a proud parent.

But when you're in your last years and your kids haven't quite gotten their acts together, I think the sadness and stress of knowing that brings on death that much quicker.

I wanted my father to feel comfort in knowing that his children and grandchildren would be all right, that someone in the family would have enough money to help out less fortunate members when necessary.

I told Puff that I wanted my father to see me make this dream come true, and to do that, I needed him to release my album. If he didn't, I was going to see my lawyer about breaking the chains that enslaved me to Bad Boy for life.

CHAPTER 21

Road to Morocco

I tried to convince Puff that my album could turn things around for Bad Boy in the same way as debut albums by Mase and Black Rob. Sensing that I was fed up with his stalling, Puff promised to make arrangements for me to get into the studio to record an album. He said that I would have a wait a few months, though, because BMG might sever its ties to Bad Boy.

I took him at his word since there had been rumblings for weeks that BMG was looking for any way it could find to drop Puff. None of his albums had sold as well as the first one, he had too many unhappy artists leaving the label, and he was beginning to release songs that Biggie had recorded but hated or left unfinished. People joked that the way he kept recycling Biggie's material, it wouldn't be long before Puff was putting out albums like "Biggie Sings the Blues" and "Biggie and Celine Dion: Duets."

In June 2002, Arista sold its half of Bad Boy back to Puff and washed their hands of him. LA Reid wanted to keep Carl Thomas, Faith Evans, and a couple of other artists in order to do justice to their flagging careers, but Puff's asking price was too high. Despite how Puff's pigheaded ways had damaged Clive Davis' career, the elderly mogul came to his rescue once again with a distribution deal.

A month later, Sauce Money and several others who worked on "No Way Out," sued Puff because they had hardly received any royalties from the 1997 album. The suit accused Puff of engaging in fraudulent activities to rip them off. Shortly after they filed suit, model Tyson Beckford sued Puff for using photos of him in Sean John Clothing ads after their contract had expired.

The most disturbing lawsuit, however, was filed by Miami-based Moore and Bode Cigars. The company granted Puff's request for permission to shoot a video in their boutique cigar factory on the condition that the cameramen refrain from shooting any footage of their propriety manufacturing process.

When company officials turned their backs, someone shot footage of the company's "secret process" of rolling cigars and then used the footage in the "Shake Ya Tailfeatha" video.

Although he promised to try to become a better Christian after he was acquitted, the lawsuits proved that he had learned nothing about treating people fairly. He was deceiving everyone, but the way he treated two women who were trying to become Bad Boy artists really stuck with me.

There was an artist signed to Bad Boy in 2000 by the name of Tammy Ruggiero that I started thinking about when I realized what he was doing to me. When the only thing that seemed to generate multiplatinum sales of R&B records was a white female artist, Puff signed one. She was about twenty-two years old at the time.

I remember when she'd come to Daddy's House to record. She would leave her infant son with her mother until she finished. She would talk about how wonderful Puff was and how proud her mother was in knowing that her daughter would soon have enough money to afford day care and anything else she needed. Months passed by, and she found out that her budget had somehow dried up.

Without a budget, there was no way for her to finish the album. She would stop by less and less often, always leaving her child with the grandmother who surely must have started losing faith. She looked sadder each time she came to the studio, and one day she just stopped coming at all.

It had to be a hard letdown not only for her and her child, but for her mother and the rest of her family and friends who were praying for her to succeed.

It didn't seem to matter to Puff that was ruining people's lives. He was preoccupied now with his new reality show on MTV called "Making the Band." The show was little more than a peek inside what really happens at Daddy's House. Basically, he would put a bunch of desperate poor black kids in a group house for a few months while they auditioned for a new rap group that he was forming.

I'll never forget Kimberly "Mysterious" Bert, the 21-year-old lady who competed for the female rap position in the second season. Not only was she very good, but she had charisma and stage presence. Anyone could tell that she was the best choice.

On one of the shows, she was moved from her upstairs bedroom to a room in the basement where musical equipment was stored. The reason behind this was because Puff felt that she was getting "too comfortable."

Another time, he had the group walk across a busy bridge just to get him a slice of cheesecake. For Puff, degrading those children was entertainment.

What the audience never knew is that Puff ran so many mind games on Mysterious that she suffered a nervous breakdown during the season finale.

"I ended up going to Bellevue that day," she told fans and reporters. "They (the Bad Boy staff) put me in the mental institution that night because I went on a rage" after she was eliminated from the competition.

People thought that she was merely being difficult during the show but it was a lot deeper than that. Mysterious had grown up in foster care. She lived in eight different foster homes in Detroit before she was eight years old, and was then placed in several homes for girls and finally a juvenile detention facility. She ran away to New York in a bid to become a rapper, ultimately crossing paths with Mary J. Blige and Carl Thomas who brought her to Puff's attention.

She didn't meet her siblings – two sisters and a brother – until she was 17 years old. When she was 19, her brother died in her arms after being shot. Even worse news came as the MTV season was wrapping up. She had to leave the show and return to Detroit because her sister Markeisha was murdered. The killer dismembered the body and threw it in a dumpster.

Although Puff seemed to welcome her back to the show, she felt like he really didn't make enough allowances for all that she had been through.

"Puff is full of shit," she said. "I felt like he betrayed me."

Because Puff was busy with lawsuits, the TV show and touring to promote his new album, I decided to wait until our tour ended to confront him one final time about my album. While I was spending all of my time on the road, Deirdre had to turn the living room of our tiny apartment into a bedroom for our son.

I was sending money home, but we still couldn't afford healthcare coverage or anything. My chasing a music career without finishing my education left me without a safety net. If I didn't make it, my future looked very dim. I was really hoping to get the album released before my father died.

My aunt called me in early September to tell me that my father's cancer had metastasized to the degree that his death could come any day. I was heart-broken. I wondered what I could do to bring some sunshine into his life that he might forget his pain for a minute.

I called Puff's office and asked if they could please send a nice flower arrangement to my father and have Puff sign the card. I tried to explain to his assistant how much it would mean to Dad and to me.

When I went to visit him on September 17, all of the nurses were coming into his room to meet Mr. Curry's "famous" son. They all thought that he was something special after reading the note from Puff that came with the flowers, and he was. He was in agonizing pain, but he seemed to forget about it every time someone came into the room and he got another chance to introduce me. Elma Kenneth Curry, my father, died the next day.

I rejoined the tour after Dad's funeral. My mother took my father's death pretty hard even though they had been apart for years. I had failed to get my album released in time to celebrate the event with my father, so I was more determined than ever to make sure that Mom lived to see that day.

More and more positive reviews from entertainment reporters came my way as the tour continued. In contrast, Puff received an increasing number of negative ones.

"The weakness of a jack of all trades is that he's the master of none," Kyle Munson wrote after we played at a popular casino in the Midwest in September. "Diddy is far from the most adept rhymer behind a microphone. His own sidekick, Mark Curry, unleashed a smoother vocal flow on Sunday."

The favorable reviews proved to be a double-edged sword. From a business standpoint, it gave Puff the perfect reason to release my album. From a rapper's standpoint, it heightened his jealousy of me. He was slipping back into the belligerent ways that led to so much trouble in 1999.

For example, Puff was at an after party for the Vogue/VH1 Fashion awards in mid-October 2002, surrounded by his security forces as usual. Actor Heath Ledger was there, too, dancing with supermodel Naomi Campbell. As Ledger and Campbell were tripping the light fantastic, Puff's guards started harassing him for "dancing too close" to Puff's table. Ledger was puzzled by their reaction and told them to take a hike. The guards were about to beat up the actor when Campbell told them to chill out. Puff idolized Campbell, so the guards backed off.

Later that month, Puff surprised everyone by announcing that we were all going to Africa in November to celebrate his 33rd birthday. As part of a plan to boost tourism to Morocco, King Mohammed VI hosted the country's largest ever publicity stunt, throwing a five-day birthday party for High Royal Excellency Puff Daddy.

More than 300 guests flew in for the party, including Naomi Campbell, Elton John, Ivana Trump, and Chris Tucker. The celebration was said to have cost over a million dollars. Some reported that all expenses were footed by the king, but others wrote that Puff actually paid the bill. Puff stayed in a palace given to the king on his 25th birthday by his father. The joint was huge, with more than 15 bedrooms and an Olympic-sized pool in the back.

It was centered on pastures of nothing but green grass with white couches scattered here and there for people to sit and enjoy watching movies on a theatre-sized screen that was on the far side of the estate. Food was prepared for us around the clock. They had food set up for us everywhere we went. We went four-wheeling one day and they set up a bar and kitchen for us outside the dirt trail.

Wolf and his girlfriend stayed in the palace as part of Puff's entourage. So did Demetrius "Meech" Flenory, head of the Black Mafia Family, and his brother Terry "Southwest T" Flenory.

I stayed at the Palmeraie Golf Palace Hotel in Morocco. The hotel situation there was a lot different from America. Double beds are twin beds pushed together with a sheet that divides them in the middle. One person lies with their head to the top, and one person lies with the head to the bottom.

Unless you're married, a man and a woman can not sleep in the same bed. In Morocco, if a person is caught in a room with a person of the opposite sex and they're not married, they get three months in jail.

I had a jovial discussion with a security guard one evening, telling him that if a person paid their money to stay in a hotel, they should have the right to bring in whomever they felt like into their room.

The security guard barely knew English and had to have someone translate what I said. I could tell by the expression on his face that he was very upset. I asked him to give me one good logical reason as to why it was a problem there in Morocco.

After going back and forth for several minutes he gave a reply that surprised me. He said that little privileges like cohabitation was one of the reasons why people left Morocco and moved to America. I thought that I could never appreciate my country more than I did after the World Trade Center attack a year earlier, but the guard's comments made me that much prouder to be an American.

I was able to put my worries behind me while I was in Morocco. But once the party was over and we were back in New York, I was determined to make Puff live up to his promise to produce my album.

Hoping to salvage both my career and Bad Boy's reputation as a place were fresh hip hop was brewed, I bought my own studio equipment so that I could record without being told when and where I could. Once I had enough songs for the album, I asked Puff one more time about the budget for my album.

"The money should be available any day now," he assured me.

Several weeks passed and I was unable to get a more definitive answer from him about an exact date. When he kept dodging the question, I got a sick feeling in my stomach.

I started calling a friend in the accounting department at Bad Boy and asking her if my budget had been approved yet. I was calling her office so much that I knew I was getting on her nerves, so one day I simply dropped by to see her.

"Mark, I hate to tell you this, but there is no budget for your album," she said as she looked sadly into my eyes. "There is no budget now and there never will be."

I instinctively gasped for air as my heart began quivering. For a minute I damn near started bawling.

"He told some of us that he never had any intentions of releasing your album," she continued. "You know by now how he operates. You are the only person here who consistently writes hits for him. If he launches your career, that'll be the end of his career."

The words "he never had any intentions of releasing your album" played over and over again in my head as I walked out of her office and out of the building. I had been warned by friends long ago that Puff would release me without ever releasing my album because his act was in essence my act. He used me to write hits for him, to teach him how to rap, and stole the majority of my publishing on top of it.

Puff will sign an artist to Bad Boy and the parent label (like Arista) will give him a budget for them. The budget goes right back to Puff because you're recording at his studio. Puff pays the producers, the writers, guest artists, technicians and everybody else out of your budget.

Puff gets a cut of money from all of those people as well because they all work for his company and he claims to help all of them to do their job. He gets a cut of everybody's publishing.

I asked him about what the accountant said and he swore up and down that it was a lie. Yet he would never agree to show me the budget that he submitted for me, would never tell me when he submitted it, and would never tell me when I could get into the studio to record.

I was around Daddy's House long enough to see how Puff burned his artists until he burned them until they burned out. I saw how G-Dep and Faith Evans turned to drugs to cope with the stress, how Mase turned to God, how Black Rob turned to crime, and how Shyne ended up in jail for putting too much faith in him.

I remained strong in my faith, in my parents, and in God, and vowed to never let Puff beat me down like that. I had chances to leave this situation, but I always felt that my mission was to stay and keep doing what I was doing until Puff's eyes were open to His great power. I didn't realize it then, but I was in the throes of a baptism by fire.

CHAPTER 22

Chaos

Despite the strong power of my faith, I grew more and more upset with Puff as time went by. I decided to return to Atlanta before I did something that both of us would regret.

I got so angry that every time he visited Atlanta I wanted to confront him. I wanted to hurt the boy real bad, do something to him to let him know that God was watching his evil and destructive ways.

I wanted to take retribution into my own hands, and I made no secret of it when I talked to my family and friends. I would get mad and vent until they grew tired of me and my complaints.

"Let go and let God," they'd say.

With no steady income from Bad Boy, I had to figure out how to earn money. Since I was regarded as a star in Atlanta, I would go to a club and just pull up and tell the bouncer to let the owner know I was there and that I would come in for a while for $500. They would pay me just like that because it was a good investment. More people would frequent the club if they thought that a celebrity was likely to drop by any day.

The only person who seemed interested in talking about the evils that Puff did was Wolf, who was also spending most of his time in Atlanta now. He was angry as well. He would complain about how he had been Puff's security for so many years and was still struggling. D-Mack and Puff were no longer friends, either, so he went back to LA.

Wolf was upset with Puff for a dozen reasons, but mainly because he had to spend his own money on attorney's fees when he was on trial with Puff and Puff was the main one in the club acting a fool.

Like Shyne, Wolf knew enough of the truth about what happened that night inside Club New York that his testimony could have sealed a conviction for Puff not only for what happened inside the club in December 1999, but for other things that might have interested an ambitious prosecutor. Wolf knew where Bad Boy's skeletons were buried.

One night in 2002 Puff threw a party at Visions nightclub in Atlanta and things got ugly between him and Wolf. They were arguing when Puff got right up in Wolf's face and started talking about how much power he had over him and what he could do to ruin him if he wanted.

When Wolf had heard enough of the blowhard, he grabbed Puff by the collar and pushed and pulled him all over the club. He mopped the floor with Puff. When he finally let Puff go, Puff started talking about payback. Once he left, everyone applauded because Puff was way overdue for a good ass-whipping.

Puff left Atlanta and didn't return for months. When he did, he was with a new friend, a man who was also a friend of mine and Wolf's as well: Meech, head of the Black Mafia Family. When Puff was with Meech, it was understood that neither Wolf nor anyone else could touch him. Meech had just started his own record label and was relying on Puff to educate him.

For his 2003 summer vacation, Puff rented a 181-foot luxury yacht once owned by Christina Onassis. He paid $40,000 per day. I wasn't invited, but friends told me all about it. Accompanied by Meech and others, he sailed the waters of the Mediterranean. Puff and Meech were shooting the breeze one day when Puff started bragging about how much money he had and how many houses he had and how his artists had made him rich for life.

"Yeah, you have money," Meech replied with a stern look on his face, "but everybody else around you is broke. Everybody around me has money."

The funny thing about that conversation is that Puff was being sued at that very time by the main person who made Bad Boy successful: Kirk Burrowes.

Burrowes had been forced out the company in 1998 but had remained quiet because Puff promised to make things right. After five years of waiting, Burrowes concluded that Puff had been lying to him all along.

In the July 2003 lawsuit filed in New York, Burrowes revealed for the first time how Puff had come into his office seven years earlier wielding a baseball bat. Burrowes stated that as attorney Kenny Meiselas looked on, Puff demanded that Burrowes sign his twenty-five percent share of Bad Boy over to him.

To substantiate his claims of Puff's dark side, Burrowes also implicated Puff in the 1995 shooting of Big Jake in Los Angeles. The killing was done by members of a group known as the "enterprise," Burrowes charged, who sought "to gain power, recognition, fame and financial gain through acts and threats involving murder, mayhem and extortion."

Burrowes alleged that there was evidence linking Puff to the murder of Tupac Shakur in 1996. This charge interested federal investigators because they were already exploring Puff's relationship with

Walter "King Tut" Johnson, the main suspect in the shooting of Tupac at Quad Studios in 1994.

Predictably, Puff and his high-priced lawyers dismissed the lawsuit as fantasy.

"Burrowes hasn't been employed for seven years," Puff told reporters, "and now he makes up a fictional story for financial gain." And the media, as usual, swallowed Puff's reply without even one person asking him why so many people had claimed in recent years to have been threatened or assaulted by the record mogul.

The next five months passed by with procedural matters in the case, so Puff went on partying as usual.

Then the damnedest thing happened. Instead of launching a secret investigation to determine whether Bad Boy was a fraud factory as Burrowes alleged in his lawsuit, the government launched a secret investigation against Burrowes.

Instead of investigating charges that Puff was involved in crimes like racketeering and witness tampering, a grand jury indicted Burrowes for money laundering and witness tampering.

Many suspected that the tentacles of Puff's white bosses were behind the downfall of Burrowes. Shortly after the criminal case against him ended, the New York courts dismissed his lawsuit against Puff not because it lacked merit, but because he had failed to file the case in time to beat RICO's (Racketeer Influenced and Corrupt Organizations Act) statute of limitations. Puff's amazing teflon-coated technicolor dreamcoat had saved him once again.

I walked into Justin's restaurant on a Martini Monday in early November and spotted Wolf eating dinner. The minute I joined him at his table, Lamont "Riz" Girdy came in. Riz had been living in New York until recently.

I hadn't seen Riz in over a year. That last time I did was in New York. He was working at Daddy's House. Riz told me that he was going through some court issues in North Carolina at the time, so Puff gave him a job in order to show the court that he was gainfully employed.

Riz said that the year of being with Puff on a weekly basis was the longest year in his life. His court battle was over.

"I woke up one morning as realized that I had to get away from him because he was making me corny." Wolf and I laughed because we knew exactly what Riz was talking about. Puff is such a poseur that it gets on your nerves real bad if you hang around him too much at one time.

They asked me to stick around because they were going to a strip club as soon as they finished dining. Vee came into Justin's as we were leaving, so the four of us went to Magic City. Wolf and Riz went on stage to get a lap dance from the fine ladies while Vee and I egged them on from the bar.

I began to feel a little out of place because at the time I didn't have any money, and a strip club is no place to be if you don't have money. It defeats the whole purpose of being there. The women kept asking me if I wanted a dance and I kept having to say: "Not right now. Maybe later."

Wolf and Riz were spending big money. I thought that one of them would give me a few Benjamins but they were too busy celebrating to notice that I was broke. I finally decided to leave. I walked over to the stage and told them, shook their hands and left.

Just as I was drifting off to sleep a few hours later I heard a loud noise. It was Coolie, and old friend from LA, knocking frantically at five o'clock in the morning.

When I opened the door, he told me to throw on some clothes because we had to leave right away.

"What's goin' on?" I asked nervously.

"Wolf and Riz got shot," he said as he started crying. "They're dead."

I was shocked and choked up. I felt like I was in a trance. All the memories that I had of them played on a screen projector in my mind. I threw on an old Bad Boy shirt that I wear around the house and we left. When we got to the crime scene, police were searching and bagging evidence. I just couldn't believe that they were dead.

"I was just with them a couple of hours ago," I kept repeating to no one in particular.

You could see the bullet casings outlined on the concrete and police were washing away the blood with pressured water. A reporter approached me after noticing that my T-shirt read "P Diddy and the Family."

He asked if I knew the two who were killed. At the time I didn't know what to think or say or do, so I didn't answer and just walked away.

I later found out what happened. After they left Magic City, Riz went with Wolf to a gym where Wolf always worked out. They lifted weights for an hour or so and then went to another strip club called Chaos.

There was a reason why Wolf was out so late that night. He was looking for his girlfriend whom someone had told him was on the town with one of Meech's close friends. Wolf ran into Meech inside the club and asked him why he didn't tell him that his girl was running around with one of Meech's men.

"Damn, Wolf," Meech said. "You know that you and me are tight, so why are you letting a bitch come between us? We have no business being here arguing about someone who's disrespecting you. Your girl is being disrespectful because she should have told my boy that she was your bitch."

She may have been a bitch to Meech because she was "an exotic dancer," but to Wolf she was a very special lady. It was the same woman whom he had taken to Morocco and everywhere else in recent years. He was deeply in love with her, so he got offended by Meech referring to her that way and they began to scuffle. Security rushed over, broke them up, and then ordered Wolf to leave.

Wolf's anger intensified as he ranted outside the club. Riz tried to persuade Wolf to leave, but he was too worked up to even think about it. By this time, someone had gone inside to tell Meech that Wolf was fuming and that there might be trouble.

Chaos

When the club closed, Meech walked with a group of friends to their vehicles. Wolf appeared out of the darkness and walked into the street holding two guns.

"So, Meech," Wolf said, "you're just going to disrespect me like that?"

All of a sudden Wolf and Riz started shooting toward Meech's group. A witness said that Meech and his crew starting returning fire. When it was over, Meech had been wounded twice in the buttocks. Wolf and Riz were dead.

Riz didn't have a beef with Meech. Like Big Jake, he was just a friend who died over loyalty. I attended their funerals in New York where Puff praised them as "brothers" and then I went back to Atlanta. I regarded Meech as a good friend and I knew Wolf and Riz as friends, so the tragedy was pretty tough on me.

Meech was charged with two counts of homicide but was soon released for lack of evidence indicating that he actually had done any shooting. I was in Justin's when he first got out and the first place he came to eat was there. He was wearing a suit, so I assumed that he had just come from court.

I didn't want to leave because he would have gotten the impression that my friendship with Riz and Wolf had ended my friendship with him. He asked me to come outside and talk with him.

"First off, I don't feel like I owe nobody an explanation," he began as we looked eye to eye, but I know what you're going through so I'm gonna try to set you straight about this shit."

"I knew Wolf just like you did," he continued. "What happened that night hurt me also but Wolf was trying to take my life."

For I while I thought that there would be repercussions but things remained quiet. Meech's brother Tee went to New York and reportedly gave money to the families of Wolf and Riz and to some of their boys not only as a gesture of regret but also to prevent a bloodbath. Meech got upset with Tee about that because he felt that it was a case of an eye for an eye and a case of self-defense.

Burrowes and his attorneys had a different version of what happened that night. Wolf and Riz were killed on November 11. Wolf was scheduled to testify before a federal judge in New York the following week in the lawsuit that Burrowes had filed against Puff a year earlier.

"Anthony Jones would have been a key witness," a lawyer for Burrowes said.

I had barely gotten the murders out of my mind when I received more bad news. My mother had fallen ill and had to retire from the gas station where she had been working for 14 years. I had called her from all over the world during my travels with the Bad Boy family and she always sounded so happy. Occasionally, she would tell me that she was having some minor stomach pains when I asked about her health.

I didn't really make much of her reply at that time. I just figured that she was saying that in order to hear me lecture her about taking care of herself. I guess all parents like to be given advice by their adult children every once in a while in order to make sure that they really are adult-minded and not still thinking like children.

What she thought was an ulcer or periodic severe stomach ache turned out to be colon cancer. She went through chemotherapy but complained that it was almost as bad as the disease. It made her weak, it made her fingernails turn black, and it made her hair fall out. The two things on the body that the average woman cares most about are their hair and their nails, and my mother was no exception.

She was rushed to the hospital on the first day of March 2004. The doctor came out and told us that she probably only had a few days left to live. I was flat broke at the time. I knew family members would be coming into town, and that many of them thought that I was wealthy because they had seen me on TV with Puff.

I called Puff and asked him if he could advance me some of the money that I would receive later from my publishing. I hadn't really talked to him much since Wolf and Riz died, but I thought that he would at least return my call when he heard why I had called. I got no response.

When I told a friend about my predicament, he said that he could give me five pounds of marijuana to sell and keep the money. The reefer was from his personal cache, he said, so he wouldn't get in trouble for not collecting the money for it.

I know that sounds crazy, risking my freedom to get money just so relatives wouldn't realize how broke I was, but that's how hazy my thinking was at the time. When you're adore your mother, her death can make your mind really do a number on you.

I left the hospital that night and headed towards Myrtle Beach, South Carolina. A friend that I grew up with told me that if I could make it to Myrtle Beach he would be able to sell all of it. I drove all night in order to get back to my mother as quickly as I could.

My friend sent his contact to my hotel room around seven o'clock the next morning. The guy looked at the weed, smelled it and then said that he didn't want it. I didn't have time to argue, so I put the weed back into the bag and packed for home. I thought the sale was a sure thing, and consequently had no money on me. I didn't have a dollar for gas. My friend gave me one hundred fifty dollars.

"Your mom was always so nice to me," he said.

I made it back to Atlanta on March 3. Mother died the next day. I didn't have enough money to pay for the accommodations of relatives or even to pay for all of the uncovered funeral expenses. I'm sure they must have wondered what happened to all that "big-time celebrity money" that I was rumored to have. If they only knew.

When my father died, I went to Puff and told him that I wanted to at least let my mother live long enough to hold my first album in her hands.

"Don't worry about it, Mark," he said. "I promise you it'll be out way before then."

CHAPTER 23

Book 'em

Bad Boy. The words hovered over my head like storm clouds as 2004 slipped away. I wondered whether Puff remembered about his promise to me when he learned of my beloved mother's passing.

After she died, I lost most of my desire to even be released on the Bad Boy label. I had fought him for so long that I finally concluded that it was one battle that I could not win. I called my lawyer to see if he could talk to Puff about releasing me from my contract.

I was far from the only one that Puff had left hanging, though. Random House sued him in February 2005 over the autobiography that he failed to deliver. The company stated that it wouldn't have sued had he returned the $350,000 advance, but Puff had kept promising them for five years that the book was coming. When he refused to cooperate with Mikal Gilmore, who was relying on money from the book to settle his debts, the writer had to file for bankruptcy.

In April, Puff effectively ended his stake in the Bad Boy label. He sold the company to Warner Music but remained CEO of Bad Boy. The deal netted him another $30 million. He settled his problems with Random House and kept on stepping.

In August, he was in the news again after British tabloids ran a story about him allegedly breaking Kim Porter's nose during a brawl on a yacht in St. Tropez. The newspaper reported that people heard them arguing about two o'clock in the morning, and some were awakened five hours later by screaming.

Puff claimed that people were mistaken about hearing them arguing and about Kim screaming. He said that they enjoyed a quiet evening, but that the boat rocked as they were going inside and Kim tripped on a rug, which caused her to fall and hit her nose on a table. Whatever happened, everyone agreed that Puff summoned a plastic surgeon to the yacht to fix the damage. Despite all the hurt that this man had caused people, the media almost always accepted his side of the story.

I started jotting down my thoughts about my life with Bad Boy and before I knew it I had written over 80 pages. I decided to write a book about the decade that I spent with the label, exposing the good and the bad. I told a few people about the book, knowing full well that they would tell Puff.

Maybe he would try to deal with me fairly if he knew that I was going to air his dirty laundry. In August 2006 I got a call from Harve Pierre. Harve said that Puff wanted to talk with me about my plans for the book.

Writing turned out to be therapeutic. It helped me to remove those lingering clouds. As I finished writing it, I felt like a man coming home from doing ten years in prison. So even though I initially considered the book as leverage, it had become something far more important.

"Do you still want to fight me, Mark Curry?" is how he began the telephone conversation.

"Do I *still* want to fight you? What makes you think I ever wanted to fight you?" I said. "I don't want to fight you."

"About seven people told me that you weren't fucking around with me no more and that you gonna write a book to tell people about how I treat my artists and shit. I don't know whether to punch them in the face or what 'cause I know they lyin' on you."

That was meant to tell me that he was my friend, but it also implied that people who "lied on him" could get hurt. He said that he was going to be doing some shows and wanted to know if I could come back on the road with him. He said that it wasn't one of those free "Homey" deals but rather a job with a check waiting for me each week.

Naturally, I wanted to refuse, but financial problems and my faith in people prevented me from doing so. I wanted to accept the offer just to see whether he was trying to apologize for how he had derailed my career and our friendship. If he was genuinely remorseful, I even contemplated changing my mind about writing the book.

We were supposed to talk in greater detail about my new gig when I got to New York. But when I arrived, he was rehearsing for the 2006 NFL kickoff and wrapping up a new album titled "Press Play."

When I walked into the rehearsal hall, I took a seat and studied the band that he had assembled for the event. The children were sensational. Each of them had been borrowed from someone else's band. Some were from Jill Scott's band and some were from R. Kelly's band and so on and so fourth.

I tried to make rehearsals fun by learning all of the kids' names and horsing around with them to ease the tension. That's what I do: I love to bring laughter into tense situations. Many of the band members had no money, and the kids were sometimes hungry. I would give some of them money for lunch or dinner or whatever. No one ever actually asked, but I could see who wasn't eating when everybody else was and I could tell who was hungry, so I gave to those who had the look. They appreciated me for that. I knew how it felt to be hungry around Puff and being too awestruck or intimidated to say anything.

One day Puff told me to meet him at his condo after rehearsal so we could talk things over. His condo in New York overlooks Central Park. All of the windows offered views of the park. People said that he loved that condo so much because he could see the area where his father was killed.

Puff started rattling on about all of his plans for the new album, about how much he spent for the condo and everything else. He was too keyed up to even remember why he asked me there. After several attempts to get him on the topic, I gave up because he was trying to talk and pack for a trip to Philly at the same time.

They handed out checks on last day of rehearsal. Everyone got a check but me. I asked a manager about it.

"Mark," he said, "I didn't want to offend you by offering you what everybody else gets, I know you have a special deal going on with Puff so I'm just waiting on him to tell me what to pay you."

We went to Miami for the show. Puff and I still hadn't sat down to talk. I wanted to tell him about my book. After rehearsal the day of the show, he told me to meet him at his house on Star Island, which is about 5 minutes from South Beach. I rode my scooter over.

I pulled up to a house that looked similar to the Hotel Atlantis in the Bahamas. Puff bought this house from Tommy Mottola for $25 million, which was about five times as much as Mottola paid. He seemed to idolize the guy.

When I walked into that house I wondered how someone who calls me his friend can live in so many million dollar homes but pay me so sporadically that my own home was in foreclosure.

They still hadn't gotten my money situation worked out after Puff's performance was over and everyone was ready to head back home. I at least wanted to get my money before I left. If I went home empty-handed my wife was gonna flip out. She already didn't feel too comfortable about me working with him again. The last thing I needed to do was come home as broke as when I left. I had to stay in New

York for two extra days to complete my mission. The label didn't want to pay for my hotel so I had to pay for it out of my paycheck.

Before I left New York, I paged Puff one last time. I told him that I was going back and if it was possible for us to continue to work I would appreciate it because I needed some income in order to get my life together. I told him that I was about to lose my home and that bill collectors were hounded me to death. Again, no response.

I guess he only needed me to help him get through those live shows and to shore up his confidence for completing the album.

Friends who didn't know how bad things were between us asked me to help them arrange a Super Bowl party in Detroit with Puff as a special guest. I wanted to refuse but of course I was too desperate to turn my back on it.

When I called him to discuss their request, he said that he wanted $100,000 per night. After he signed the contract I gave him a check for $200,000. Under the terms of the contract, he was supposed to appear each night for one and a half hours, from half past midnight until two o'clock.

He came Friday and met his obligations. However, he arrived on Sunday 11:15 pm and only stayed for thirty minutes. After that he rushed out and hopped on a flight to Atlanta. The promoter must have spent over a half-million dollars for this event. They built a club in an open lot for the event and called it "Daddy's House." The club was incredible. Puff was on an elevated VIP balcony that overlooked everything.

At first he and his managers doubted that I could pull off the event. They didn't believe it could be done in the way that I had described it. When Puff walked in and saw that it was as said I would be, he never once said thanks. I could see resentment in his eyes.

The promoters of the event were from Detroit, a major city for gangsters. These guys don't like being ripped off. So when it was time for me to get paid for bringing Puff to town, I knew that there was going to be trouble.

They complained that Puff's early departure hurt their chances to collect on the money they spent to promote the event. Since I had paid

Puff in advance, they told me that I would have to collect my fee from him.

I told Deirdre when I left for Detroit that I would be coming back home with at least ten thousand dollars, and now I was going home broke. When I relayed their complaints to Puff, he said that it wasn't his problem and that he wasn't giving me a dime.

"You need to get your money from the promoters," he wrote in an e-mail sent via his Blackberry.

As I went home penniless, I thought about how nearly every artists signed to Puff's label had also ended up penniless, in jail, on drugs, or dead. Any artist who trusted him ended up getting burned and Puff laughed all the way to the bank.

If you run a check on ASCAP or one of the other web sites that show who owns the publishing rights to certain songs, you will find that Puff's name appears on over 250 songs even though I don't ever recall him writing a single one. I do recall him changing one word here and adding an electronic cymbal there, but nothing that constitutes contributing within the meaning of copyright laws.

Puff has victimized as many people with deceptive contracts and creative bookkeeping as his father did with drugs. I don't pretend to know the exact number, but this book offers a pretty good sample. Puff should have no trouble understanding it. He is, after all, the Master Sampler.

EPILOGUE

Fallen Angel

When D-Mack first introduced me to Puff, I just knew that music was my calling. Using the musical talent that God blessed me and my ancestors with, I felt like I had a special gift that God wanted me to use to bring joy to others. When I signed the contract, I thought that God was going to work through Puff to lead my life in the right direction.

I was always thrilled to perform on stage, and I enjoyed the camaraderie of being off stage with fellow artists, friends, and fans. I kept a mental note of all those people who supported me from the beginning to the end of my years at Bad Boy because I figured that I would get a chance to pay all of them back one day.

I was instrumental in saving the Bad Boy label after Christopher "Notorious BIG" Wallace was slain and Puff knows that. I was instrumental in Bad Boy's fulfilling its contractual commitment to the makers of the movie, "Godzilla," and Puff knows that. I taught him how to rhyme and how to move when you rhyme. He knows that.

If you look at all of the early hit songs that Puff had, you will find my name on most of them.

I am not saying any of this to brag, but merely to point out what too much faith in another person has netted me. Although Puff sold Bad Boy and sold out the real "bad boys" of hip hop, he remains a multimillionaire whom many people think is a genuinely good guy.

But let's look at those who trusted him. I bought a home for my wife and child after Puff promised to release my album in 2005. He actually went on radio and told fans that I was in the studio finishing up my debut album. You can verify this by simply typing in my name and his name in Google or other search engines, or checking some of the Bad Boy sites for fans.

Last year, I lost my home to foreclosure just like thousands of other American families who placed too much faith in their fellow man, like the sweet-talking lady at the mortgage refinancing company. Today I am homeless and still driving a 1992 Honda Accord that I bought at auction five years ago. I still cannot afford health insurance for my son, my wife or myself.

But as Gloria Gaynor sings, I'll survive. Guys like Puff who grow up with a silver spoon in their mouth take so much for granted. They think that all those young people in the ghetto and the barrios have nothing better to do than join gangs and get into fights so they can end up as a crime statistic.

Guys like Puff don't realize that no one in his right mind really wants to be a player or a con artist or a thug or any of those stereotypes that do nothing but keep black men on the bottom of the economic totem pole.

If you reflect on the careers of any of the gangster rappers – even going back to the beginning with men like Dolomite in the early 1960s and the Last Poets in the early 1970s when hip hop was born – you will discover that most of them died broke or still live hand-to-mouth. The major exceptions which come to mind are two stone "cold" rappers: Ice-T and Ice-Cube.

Ice-T claims that he was a big-time pimp once upon a time but the evidence is thin. He gained national attention after recording a song called "Cop Killer" which was in response to police brutality in ghettos. But when Hollywood came calling with an ironic offer – the producers of a hit crime drama wanted him to play a cop – all Ice-T said was "show me the money." He has been a better role model playing a fictional cop than he was during his days advocating the murder or real ones or trying to be Iceberg Slim Jr.

Ice Cube is an artist who grew up in the ghetto and whose lyrics had young black men thinking about revolutionary changes in America and how racism reinforces economic oppression. Once again, though, Hollywood came knocking with one of those offers that most people can't refuse.

You won't hear him talking about revolutionary changes anymore. But you might see him paying a couple of poor Latinos to fix up his vacation home in his latest movie. I'm not knocking it, just stating how the tables turn and people change when you give people options and opportunities. Like Malcolm X said, if you put enough cream in your coffee, pretty soon you won't even know that the coffee was ever there. People should be able to change for the better without selling their souls.

Men like Ice Cube and Ice-T and me know the real reason why the message of hip hop got away from revolutionary change ideas and reverted to Civil War era ideas when black people used the "N word" to refer to themselves. It's social mathematics which goes like this: If a brave slave like Sojourner Truth takes one step toward freeing black Americans, a freed slave's son will one day take two steps freeing others all over the world. Truth plus activism equals liberty.

Hip hop began as music that young black people embraced because it addressed the ills that have oppressed them and their people for hundreds of years. Today it is a music that young white people embrace for reasons that still are not clear.

Someone should tell them that myths to the contrary, there is no glory in barricading your baby's crib with screens to prevent rats from biting her during the night. There is nothing cool about having to eat "sugar sandwiches" for lunch because all Mom could afford to buy with her last food stamps was a loaf of bread and a small box of sugar.

There is no glory in carrying a knife or a gun and risking being arrested because you are afraid of being jumped by another kid who wants to jump you in order to join a gang of kids sticking together to avoid being jumped.

I still cringe every time a young white kid pulls up to next to me at a stoplight with a song bleeping the "N word" blasting from his radio or when I pass by two Asian kids at the mall and hear them pretending to be gangsters by calling each other "my nigga."

If people like Puff really understood the hip hop culture, they would be out in the street picketing his own record label and sending petitions to Congress to demand that record executives stop turning away black artists who refuse to sing about drugs and violence or refuse to rap about being pimps and killing or indulging in all the other vices that have ruined minority communities.

Music with a positive message has just as much right to be heard as music with a negative one. Stop locking out brothers who want to rap about correcting social ills.

Yes, I wrote about those things once upon a time. But I was young and unaware of the cultural ramifications of what I was doing. I had no children at the time, so I didn't think about the impact of the music on children until I had a son of my own. I didn't think about all the senseless violence mentioned in the song in those days.

But today, when I visit my friend Chris who took me to the Million Man March and who supported my musical ambitions from the beginning, I think about those lyrics. I think about them because a young man who wanted to earn street credibility shot Chris at close range two years ago, leaving him paralyzed.

I think about the guy Eddie who sold drugs to Bobby Brown right out in the open at nightclubs in Atlanta. Eddie was selling death, if you recall. He ended up selling one death too many: someone killed him.

I think about Jay-D, the wild and crazy guy who went up against the Colombian drug lords and who would fight anybody at the drop of a hat. So here's a shout out to you, Jay-D, because I know that you will read this book many times while you finish serving your 80-year sentence stemming from a shootout with state troopers. And I think about Meech, who was recently incarcerated after pleading guilty to multiple drug offenses. Say what you will, but any brother who can handle an operation that large is a genius. Maybe God will help him use his natural abilities to straighten out the lives of a lot of the young cats who idolize him.

When people asked me why I chose to refer to Puff as "the devil," I surprised many of them by saying that I really believe he is a devil – of sorts.

People have no problem thinking of certain other people as earthly angels, even though they don't use that term per se. But when we call someone or designate someone as a saint, aren't we really saying that she was an angel compared to other people?

When we look at people who have devoted their lives to helping their fellow man despite their own troubles or poverty or ill health or whatever, aren't we separating them out for special status among humans? Of course we are.

So if we think of people like Edgar Cayce and Mother Theresa and Mohandas Gandhi and Dr. Martin Luther King Jr. as saints among mortals, why can't we accept the idea that people like Hitler and Count Dracula the Impaler and Nero were devils among men?

God removed Puff's daddy from this earth when Puff was only two years old. That was a heavy burden for a child to carry. But the Holy Bible reminds us that the sins of the father are often visited upon the children or even the grandchildren.

In selling lethal drugs to the desperate people of Harlem and the Bronx, Melvin Combs ruined families, forced people to give up their jobs in order to feed a drug habit, and deprived children of their parents due to fatal drug overdoses or lifelong incarceration.

But He also blessed Puff with the means to correct the sins of his father. He placed Puff in a position whereby he could have shared his wealth with scores of poor talented artists who only wanted an opportunity to escape poverty and to pull as many others as possible out of poverty in the process. Puff made us promises that made us believe God was using him as His Instrument when in fact it was Satan who was using Puff.

I was always bothered by the contract that I signed with D-Mack and Puff at the start of my career. I knew something was wrong with it, but I was desperate to get signed. I didn't understand just how bad the deal was until years later when I read an article in *Billboard* by an entertainment lawyer.

In July 1999, Bob Donnelly wrote that production deal contracts being used by Bad Boy and similar record labels were worse that the contracts signed by black artists in the 1950s that left most of them destitute at the end of their careers while white record company executives became filthy rich from royalties that should have been going to the artists.

If you've seen the recent movie, "Cadillac," a fictional account which glosses over how black singers were mistreated by Chess Records founder Leonard Chess, you have some idea of what Donnelly is talking about. A Cadillac car in exchange for millions in future royalty payments is a deal designed by the Devil himself.

"The production agreement is the single most regressive and anti-artist contract introduced in the music industry during the last two decades," Donnelly writes. "While the days of cheating unsuspecting bluesmen may be over – I'm sorry to say the days of ripping off naive rappers and hip hoppers is in its ascendancy. The only difference is that this time it's often black managers, producers and record companies who are taking advantage of black artists (...frequently with the assistance of white music lawyers)."

Donnelly spells out what happened to me, G-Dep, Shyne, Biggie, Black Rob, and all of the other poor young black men who trusted Puff and his rich old white lawyers.

It took me a long time to understand that, but I take comfort in knowing that I have prevented some of my friends and other budding artists from agreeing to any deal where someone wants a percentage of the gross instead of the net. Anytime someone tells you that they want to be paid from your gross amount, tell them that they are "gross" and to get the hell out of your face because they are trying to rob you.

Puff's timidity as a young adult prompted him to forge an image of himself as a gangster. Young brothers like Biggie, Shyne, Mase, and G-Dep knew that there is no real glamour in being a thug, so they came to Puff in hopes that he would rescue them from that fate.

Instead of rescuing them, Puff demanded that they pretend to be the very thing that they wanted to escape: an uneducated black man feared and reviled by the public.

When I signed with Bad Boy, my mother was as happy as someone who had just discovered a gold mine. I can see the smile on her face now as she watched me on television. I can hear my father's voice saying how proud he was of me being signed to a major record label.

I am happy that Puff gave me and chance to succeed in music, but I'm unhappy that the only reason he did so was to develop his own career as a rapper.

I'm happy that my wife stood by me through all those years because her faith in me gave me the strength to keep writing hit songs, but I'm unhappy because Puff took those hit songs for himself and prevented me from taking my talent elsewhere. My wife entrusted our future to me, but my reliance on Puff made my promises to her and Mark Jr. end up as lies.

My music comes from my heart. It's a symbol of my life and of the human experience. When I started to realize what kind of person Puff really was, I was doing some serious spiritual rebuilding. When I reflected on the time that I had invested in him, I felt lost and alone.

I still don't know why God put my life on the same road next to Sean John Combs, and I may never know. I do hope that in writing this cautionary tale about what really happens inside the music business, I will prevent at least one young man or woman from signing a record deal before consulting with a counselor or lawyer who is independent of the record companies. If only one person hears my message and avoids the sharp curve in the road where my own hopes and dreams crashed and died, that will be testament enough to God's greatness and to my true mission in life.

Through prayer, I have finally vanquished the hard feelings I harbored for Puff. As my father told me once, the only way to beat the devil is to love the "hell" out of him.

The title of this book is based on a story that a minister used to tell us in church. A parishioner came to him one day and asked if a man would burn in hell if he had an affair with the married woman next door.

"Well, son," the minister replied, "you may not burn in Hell, but you'll suffer burns on your hands or feet or somewhere because you can't dance with the devil and not get burned."

"The Good Lord," he continued, "doesn't ask much of His spoiled children. All he wants us to do is to follow the Ten Commandments. There are a lot of commandments, you know, but God makes it easy on us by reducing the number to just ten. One of them says that Thou Shall Not Covet Thy Neighbor's Spouse. So if you've already had that affair, you've violated God's top ten list. Every time you violate God's top ten, you're dancing with the Devil himself."

Bibliography

BOOKS:

Brown, Ethan. *Queens Reigns Supreme: Fat Cat, 50 Cent, and the Rise of the Hip Hop Hustler*. (New York: Anchor Books, 2005)

Chang, Jeff. *Can't Stop, Won't Stop: A History of the Hip-Hop Culture*. (New York: St. Martin's Press, 2005)

Ro, Ronin. *Bad Boy: The Influence of Sean "Puffy" Combs on the Music Industry*. (New York: Simon & Schuster, 2001)

Sullivan, Randall. *Labyrinth: A Detective Investigates the Murders of Tupac Shakur and Notorious B.I.G., the Implications of Death Row Records' Suge Knight, and the origins of the Los Angeles Police Scandal.* (New York: Grove Press, 2002)

Wallace, Voletta. *Biggie. Voletta Wallace Remembers Her Son.* (New York: Atria Books, 2005)

PERIODICALS:

"13 Men, 5 Women Are Indicted Here on Heroin Charge," *New York Times*, October 21, 1972, p. A26.

"2 Held Without Bail in Bribe Linked to East Harlem Slaying," *New York Times*, January 18, 1972, p. A35.

Alexander, Keith L. "Combs Admits Major Mistake; Airing of Music Video Led to Altercation," *USA Today,* June 24, 1999, p. B03.

Allen, Angela C. "Beaten Record Exec: I'll See Puffy Behind Bars," *New York Post*, May 21, 1999, p.14.

Andelman, David. "Shooting Case Could Topple Puffy's Empire; $300 Million-a-Year Industry Relies on Combs at the Helm to Keep it Hip-Hopping," *New York Daily News*, February 4, 2001, p. 26.

Anson, Sam Gideon and Charles Rappleye. "Murder Was the Case: Notorious B.I.G. Shot Down at 24," *Village Voice*, March 18, 1997, p. 40.

"Atlanta Rappers Arrested in Drug Raid, *United Press International*, June 14, 2006.

"Arista Continues Hot Streak with Sixth Consecutive Record Year," *Business Wire*, July 20, 1998.

Bastone, William. "No Sugar Daddy," *Village Voice*, March 3, 1998, p. 51.

Bellville, Rebecca. "Suspect Charged in Murder of AU Alum [Tyrone "Tymex" Birchett]," *The Eagle* [American University], February 5, 2004.

Benza, A.J. "No Victoria Victor," *New York Daily News*, August 6, 1995, p. 28.

"Best-Selling Records of 1998," *Billboard*, January 30, 1999.

Blankstein, Andrew. "Lawyers for Rapper's Kin Outline Case; Attorneys for the Family of Slain Star Notorious B.I.G. Say They Plan to Present Evidence in Lawsuit that Links LAPD Officer to Shooting," *Los Angeles Times*, June 21, 2005, p. B03.

_____. "LAPD Hid Claims, Judge Says; Bratton Denies, However, That an Informant's Statements Linking Officers to Notorious B.I.G.'s Slaying Were Concealed on Purpose," *Los Angeles Times*, July 8, 2005, p. B01.

Bolden, James. "Cops Overreacted, Says Rapper Tupac Shakur's Attorney; Rapped Held in Shooting of Two Police Officers, *Los Angeles Sentinel*, November 17, 1993, p. 1.

"Bond Set for Man Accused in Death of P. Diddy's Former Bodyguard," *Associated Press*, November 27, 2003.

Boucher, Geoff and Chuck Philips. "Rap Music Crowd Shrugs Off Latest Shooting Incident; Suge Knight, Wounded at Party, Is Expected to Recover," *Los Angeles Times*, August 29, 2005, p. A08.

Boyd, Herb. "Two Rap Groups Agree to End KISS-FM Fomented Dispute," *New York Amsterdam News*, May 22, 1993, p. 4.

"Bronx and Westchester Raids Net $6 Million in Uncut Heroin," *New York Times*, December 16, 1971, p. A64.

Bronson, Fred. "A Fresh Chart Page for Jimmy," *Billboard*, June 27, 1998.

Browning, Dan. "Money Launderer For Gang Gets 9 Years; The High-Level Member of the Shotgun Crips Took a Plea Deal for Laundering Profits from Twin Cities Drug Deals," *Minneapolis Star Tribune*, January 19, 2007.

Bruck, Connie. "The Takedown of Tupac," *New Yorker*, July 7, 1997.

"Burrowes Tapped as Bad Boy Prez, To Expand Label's Staff," *Billboard*, February 22, 1997.

Campos, Carlos. "Home of Rich and Notorious to be Razed, Much to Neighbor's relief; Five New Houses to Be Built on Site [Michael Thevis]," *Atlanta Journal-Constitution*, June 22, 1995, p. J15.

Chapman, Francesca. "Puffy Held Responsible for Deaths of Nine Fans," *Philadelphia Daily News*, January 13, 1999, p. 38.

"Combs Corrects Yacht Fight Reports," *WENN Entertainment News Wire*, August 19, 2005.

"Combs Denies the Rumors of Ties to Murder, Gangs," *Chicago Sun-Times*, May 28, 1997, p. 44.

Cook, Joan. "Father Is Cleared by Polygraph Test in 5 Jersey Deaths," *New York Times*, December 16, 1975.

Daly, Michael. "Tagged to Legacy of Violence," *New York Daily News*, March 14, 2001, p. 2.

"DEA Deals Motor City Mafia a Knockout Blow," *US Fed News*, October 25, 2005.

Donnelly, Bob. "What's the Deal with Production Deals?" *Billboard*, July 31, 1999.

Downey, Maureen. "Firm Yanks Bobby's Welcome Mat," *Atlanta Journal-Constitution*, September 7, 1994, p. B02.

Dvorak, Petula. "Music Promoter's Death Called Suspicious," *Washington Post*, December 11, 2003, p. B03.

Dwyer, Jim. "A Winner Would Say He's Sorry to Victims," *New York Daily News*, February 26, 1998, p. 6.

"Eazy E Sues Sony Music, Others," *Daily Variety*, October 16, 1992.

Elsen, Jon. "Arista Huffing and Puffing Over Puffy's $50M," *New York Post*, June 3, 1999, p. 42.

Eshun, Ekow. "The Rap Trap: Dr. Dre Helped Pioneer Hardcore Hip-Hop; Now a Millionaire Father of Two, He Says He's Turned Over a New Leaf – All That Gangsta Stuff Was Just About Marketing, Pleasing the Fans," *London Guardian*, May 27, 2000, p. 8.

Faison, Seth. "3 Officers Hurt in Shootout with Suspects in 2 Robberies," *New York Times*, January 16, 1993, p. A25.

"Federal Court Dismisses Lawsuit Filed by Jacques Agnant Alleging He was Defamed by Lyrics of Tupac Shakur Recording," *Entertainment Law Reporter*, July 1999, Vol. 21, No.2.

Finkelstein, Katherine E. "In Lengthy Closing, Prosecutor Accuses Combs of Deceit and Arrogance," *New York Times*, March 14, 2001, p. B03.

_____. "Rapper Accused of Trying to Bribe 4 Potential Witnesses," *New York Times*, February 22, 2001, p. B02.

_____. "Officers Describe Encounter with Combs," *New York Times*, February 9, 2001, p. B06.

Fitzgerald, Henry Jr. "Man Sentenced for Super Bowl Ticket Scheme," *Sun-Sentinel*, December 5, 1995, p. B03.

Fitzgerald, Jim. "New York Jail Inmate Accused of Bilking Nextel Out of 1,000 Cell Phones," *Associated Press*, August 8, 2002.

Fleischer, Matt. "Puff Daddy Keeps a Father Waiting," *New York Observer*, May 17, 1999.

Fosburgh, Lacey. "3 Police Indicted in Bribery Case; They are Accused of Taking $2,000 to Allow Suspect in Murder to Flee," *New York Times*, January 13, 1972, p. A01.
Francis, Vivienne. "Nation [of Islam] Set to Heal Rap Feud," *The Weekly Journal*, October 12, 1995.

Gardner, Ralph Jr. "What Price Puffy? The High Cost of Liberty When You're a Music Mogul Charged with Gun Possession," *New York Observer*, March 26, 2001.

Gearty, Robert. "Money-Launder Rap for P. Diddy Pal," *New York Daily News*, August 13, 2004, p. 40.

_____. "$25 Million Suit Says Puffy Went Batty," *New York Daily News*, July 1, 2003, p. 8.

Gilmore, Mikal. "Puff Daddy: The New King of Hip-Hop," *Rolling Stone*, August 7, 1997 (cover story).

Gonzalez, David. "8 Lives That Came Together, Then Were Lost in a Crush," *New York Times*, December 30, 1991, p. A01.

Gregorian, Dareh. "Diddy Bully Her? Puff Threatened Me: Ex's Lawyer," *New York Post,* July 27, 2001, p. 23.

Hanley, Robert. "Police Still Have No Clues in Killing of 5 in Bergen Family 2 Years Ago," *New York Times*, December 3, 1977, p. 51.

_____. "Three Are Suspected In Slaying of Five in Teaneck," *New York Times*, October 21, 1976, p. 81.

Hay, Carla. "Rap Execs Face Police Investigations," *Billboard*, May 1, 1999.

Helmore, Edward. "Rap's Off; Death Row, the Late Tupac Shakur's Record Label, Is Going Down in a Blaze of Gunfire, Drug-Trafficking and Money-Laundering," *London Independent*, August 29, 1997, p. 10.

Hirschberg, Lynn. "Does a Sugar Bear Bite?" *New York Times Magazine*, January 14, 1996.

Ho, Rodney. "Landlord Plans to Raze Roof at Vision; Condos to Replace Atlanta Nightclub," *Atlanta Journal-Constitution*, July 25, 2006, p. C01.

Holland, John. "Swindler Guilty of Attack on Prison Guard," *Sun-Sentinel*, September 17, 1999, B03.

Hurtado, Patricia. "Jurors Face Fatigue; End Long Day Without Verdict in Puffy Trial," *Newsday*, March 16, 2001, p. A01.

_____. "Say the Gun is Yours"; Driver Testifies Combs Offered Him a Bribe to Take the Fall," *Newsday*, February 16, 2001, p. A03.

Iverem, Esther. "A Complicated Rap; After His B.I.G. Star's Death, Mogul Puffy Combs Says He's Got Second Thoughts," *Washington Post*, March 28, 1997, p. C01.

"Jailed Robber: Agents Wanted Diddy for Tupac's Death," *WENN Entertainment Group* (news release), July 25, 2006.

Jordan, George E. "Minister Raps Gangsta Rap," *Newsday*, February 9, 1994, p. 25.

"Jury Finds in Favor of Combs in Suit," *Associated Press*, February 24, 2004.

Katz, Ian. "Death Wish; For Many, Tupac Shakur's Bloody Murder On Saturday Was as Significant as the Deaths of Other US Icons Kurt Cobain and River Phoenix," *The Guardian* (London), September 20, 1996, p. T02.

Kennedy, Dana. "Deadly Business; Tupac Shakur's Murder, Still Unsolved, Provokes the Rap World to Reexamine Itself," *Entertainment Weekly*, December 6, 1996, p. 34.

King, Jeanne. "Wounded Man is Third Witness to Testify Puffy Combs Had a Gun," *Philadelphia Inquirer*, February 8, 2001, p. D03.

"King Tut Speaks upon Tupac Shooting, Puff Daddy and Feds," King magazine, August 2001.

Lait, Matt and Scott Glover. "Ex-LAPD Officer is Suspect in Rapper's Slaying, Records Show; Police Pursue Theory That David Mack, Since Convicted of Bank Robbery, Helped Arrange Killing of Notorious B.I.G.," *Los
Angeles Times*, December 9, 1999, p. A01.

_____. "Suit Over Slaying of LAPD Officer Settled
Quietly; City Attorney Agrees to Pay $250,000 to Family in Maneuver
That Bypasses City Council," *Los Angeles Times*, May 20, 1999, p. B01.

"Leader of Shotgun Crips Sentenced in Minneapolis to Nine Years in Federal
Prison, *States News Service*, January 18, 2007.

Lebowitz, Larry. "Court Appearance Set Today for Man Charged with
Threat on Clinton," *Sun-Sentinel*, August 25, 1998, p. B01.

Leeds, Jeff and Jim Newton. "FBI Probing Rap Label for Ties to Gangs,
Drugs; Investigation of Death Row Records Began Months Before the Fatal
Shooting of Tupac Shakur," *Los Angeles Times*, September 26, 1996, p. B01.

Louis, Errol. "Bad Boy Blues; G-Dep's Ill-fated Romance with Street Life
Serves as Cautionary Tale for Kids Blinded by Bling," *New York Daily News*,
February 18, 2007, p. 37.

Lubasch, Arnold H. "Ten Found Guilty of Heroin Charge; Convicted of
Taking Part in $5 Million-A-Year Plot," *New York Times*, February 24,
1973, p. 60.

Mackenzie, Drew. "P. Diddy Had Two Rap Rivals Shot," *Daily Star*, October 4, 2003, p. 17.

"Mad Rapper Delivers A Sermon on Mount Sinai," *Spokesman Review*, June 22, 1998, p. B02.

Maull, Samuel. "Doctor Says Wounded Witness Told Him That Combs Shot Her," *Associated Press*, February 7, 2001.

Marine, Craig. "Puff Daddy; Hip-hop King Sweeps into Town, Attitude and Entourage in Tow," *San Francisco Examiner*, August 24, 1999, p. C01.

McAdams, Janine. "Combs Moves Up to VP at Uptown Records; Also Establishes His Own Label-Linked Company," *Billboard*, December 12, 1992, p. 10.

McCullough, Alphonse. "112: ATL Teens with Multiplatinum Dreams, *YSB*, October 31, 1996, p. 14.

McFadden, Robert D. "Inquiries Begin Over City College Deaths; Survivors of Tragedy Describe the Chaos in Which 8 Died," *New York Times*, December 30, 1991, p. A01.

_____. "Behind Deadly Rush at City College; Crowd Members Describe Panic, Fear and Fatal Mistakes," *New York Times*, January 22, 1992, p. B01.

_____. "No Liability Insurance at Game That Led to the Deaths of 9; More Paid for Publicity Than Security at Event, Sponsor's Lawyer Says," *New York Times*, January 3, 1992, p. B01.

Mitchell, John L. "Ex-Prosecutor Won't Be Tried in Rap Case," *Los Angeles Times*, August 12, 1997, p. B01.

Montgomery, Bill. "Rapper, Clayton Officer Bound Over; Fulton Grand Jury Will Get Assault Case," *Atlanta Journal-Constitution*, December 2, 1993, p. D03.

Muhammad, Carrie and Sabrina 2X. "Muslims Help Rappers Avoid Bloody Feud, Blasts Station," *New York Amsterdam News*, June 12, 1993.

Murray, Matthew. "FEC Clears Diddy of Wrongdoing," *Roll Call*, October 12, 2006.

Murray, Sonia. "Dallas Austin Aims for Top of Pop World by Filling the Needs of Artists and Public," *Atlanta Journal- Constitution*, June 6, 1993, p. N01.

Newman, Maria. "Organizer of Fatal Rap Event is Hip-Hop Maestro," New York Times, January 5, 1992, p. A22.

Noel, Peter. "Puffy Betrayed Me [Shyne]," *Village Voice*, March 27, 2001, p. 54.

_____. "That's Gangsta! Puff Love in the Bad Boys Family," *Village Voice*, March 14-20, 2001, p. 42.

_____. "Bad Boy Shyne," *Village Voice*, January 30, 2001, p. 25.

_____. "Big Bad Wolf; Anthony Jones Upholds the Legend of Puff Daddy's Bodyguard," *Village Voice*, February 14-20, 2001, p. 47.

_____. "Dangerous Ground; They Finally Got Biggie in LA, After an Aborted Hit in Atlanta," *Village Voice*, March 25, 1997, p. 48.

Ogunnaike, Lola and Anemona Hartocollis. "Godfather of Bling Denies He Aided Drug Ring," *New York Times*, June 17, 2006, B03.

"P. Diddy Breaks From Arista; Bad Boy Records Seeking Distributor," *Hollywood Reporter*, June 21, 2002.

"P. Diddy's Ex-Bodyguard Killed in Atlanta," *New York Beacon*, November 19, 2003, p 3.

Pearson, Ryan. "Ex-FBI Informant Says Death Row Security Chief Vowed to Get Rapper," *Associated Press*, June 22, 2005.

_____. "LA Trial to Reveal Investigation into Rapper's Unsolved Slaying," *Associated Press*, June 21, 2005.

Phillips, Chuck. "BMG Names Reid To Succeed Davis at Arista," *Los Angeles Times*, May 3, 2000, C01.

_____. "Rapper Puff Daddy to Attend One-Day Class After Guilty Plea," *Los Angeles Times*, September 9, 1999, C01.

_____. "Rapper's Family Offers Alibi in Shakur Slaying; Documents Put Notorious B.I.G. in New York, Not Las Vegas, on the Night of the Killing," *Los Angeles Times*, September 11, 2002, p. A05.

_____ "Officers May Have Seen Rap Killing; Off-duty Inglewood Police Member Was Behind Vehicle When Rap Star Notorious B.I.G. was Slain and Undercover New York Agents Were Trailing the Singer That Night, Sources Say." *Los Angeles Times*, April 23, 1997, p. B01.

_____. "Witness in B.I.G. Case Says His Memory's Bad; The Admission Comes as Trial is Set to Begin in Suit Filed by Family of Slain Rap Star Against the City," *Los Angeles Times*, June 20, 2005, p. B01.

_____. "FBI Ends Probe Into Killing of Rap Star; Bureau Discards Theory Being Pursued by Its Lead Agent Regarding Slaying of Notorious B.I.G," *Los Angeles Times,* March 11, 2005, p. B01.

_____. "LAPD Renews Search for Rapper's Killer; If New Evidence Is Found in Biggie Smalls' Death, It Could Help Police Fight His Mother's Lawsuit," *Los Angeles Times*, July 31, 2006, p. A01.

_____. "Possible Link of Puffy Combs to Fatal Shooting Being Probed; Investigators Look into Account that Identifies His Bodyguard as the Gunman." *Los Angeles Times*, January 17, 2001, p. C01.

_____. "Investigation of Rapper's Slaying Comes Up Empty," *Los Angeles Times*, December 16, 1997, p. B01.

_____. "No Proof Against Knight in Slaying, Attorney Say; Rap Executive's Lawyer Denounces Police Allegations Regarding 1997 Shooting of Notorious B.I.G."
Los Angeles Times, August 10, 1999, p. B01.

_____. "Probe of Rap Label Looks at Entrepreneur Behind Bars; Inmate Says He Helped Start Death Row Records, Which is Under FBI Scrutiny," *Los Angeles Times*, September 1, 1997, p. A01.

_____. "Tupac Shakur's Mom Sues Label for Recordings; Death Row is Accused of Running a Criminal Enterprise that Bilked Slain Rapper Out of Millions; Lawyer Denies Charges," *Los Angeles Times*, April 19, 1997, p. D01.

Philips, Chuck and Alan Abramson. "Longo to be Dismissed by DA's Office; Appearance of Conflict Created by His Family's Dealings with Rap

Mogul Suge Knight is Cited. Prosecutor Denies Wrongdoing," *Los Angeles Times*, February 23, 1997, p. B01.

_____. "Knight's Probation Revoked by Judge; Jurist Rules that Rap Mogul Was an Active Participant in Fight at Las Vegas Hotel*," Los Angeles Times*, November 27, 1996, p. B01.

_____. "Prosecutor Probed on Rap Mogul's Probation; Death Row's Suge Knight Leased House from Family of Deputy DA Monitoring His Case and Gave Daughter a Contract," *Los Angeles Times*, October 25, 1996, p. A01.

_____. "Rap Mogul's Alleged Assault on Rival Jolts the Industry," *Los Angeles Times*, April 30, 1999, p. A01.

Piccoli, Sean. "Pop Déjà vu; Sampling Evolves into Wholesale Borrowing," *Fort Worth Star-Telegram*, October 30, 1997, p. 2.

Pollack, Marc. "Soundtracks Make Smash Hits; Angels, Godzilla Go 1-2 as Movie, TV Albums Dominate Sales, *Hollywood Reporter*, June 4, 1998.

Powell, Robert Andrew. "Con Kid; Jimmy Sabatino, Self-Described Child of the Mafia, Displayed a Prodigious Talent for Confidence Games Even as a Teenager," *Miami New Times*, September 9, 1999 (cover).

"Puff Daddy Hits the Road for the Second Time with the Star-Studded No-Way Out Tour," *Business Wire*, February 18, 1998.

"Puffy and Lopez in Public Petting," *New York Post*, May 28, 1998, p. 8.

Rankin Bill. "Threat to Mayor Was Taped; Alleged Conversation between Strip Club Owner, Informant Played During Bond Hearing in   Arson Case," *Atlanta Journal-Constitution*, February 18, 2000, p. D05.

Rapper Arrested After Shooting Injures Two Police Officers, *Associated Press*, October 31, 1993.

"Rappers Partly to Blame for Death, Says Judge, "*Calgary Herald*, January 13, 1999, p. D02.

Roberts, Johnnie L. "The World of Puff Daddy; From Hip-Hop Impresario to Global Star, Sean Combs Now Works Round the Clock, Expanding His Pop-Culture Enterprises," *Newsweek*, August 17, 1998.

_____. "The Trigger Puffy Is Really Worried About," *Newsweek*, March 15, 2001.

_____. "Puffy's Piece of the Pie," *Newsweek*, October 7, 1996, p. 58.

_____. "Puffy Dodges a Bullet," *Newsweek*, March 26, 2001, p. 44.

Robertson, Anika. "Source Awards Have Hip-Hop Hosts Ed Lover, Dr. Dre," *New York Amsterdam News*, August 12, 1995, p. 23.

Rozhon, Tracie. "The Rap on Puffy's Empire," *New York Times*, July 24, 2005, Business, p. 1.

Rush, George and Joanna Molloy. "Bio Hazards Stalling Puffy's Book," *New York Daily News*, February 28, 2000.

_____. "From the Boardrooms of Rap; CEO Suge's Got Puffy Shakin'," *New York Daily News*, December 1, 1995, p. 33.

Sales, Nancy Jo. "Is Hip-Hop's Jeweler on the Rocks?" *Vanity Fair*, November 2006, p. 204.

Sampey, Kathleen. "Burger King Tunes in DiddyTV," *Adweek*, October 11, 2006.

Sanchez, George B. "Divorce Battle Over Who Gets $107 Million Suit Settlement; Coupled Claimed to Have Helped Found Death Row Records," *Monterey County Herald*, September 20, 2005, Z-News.

Scott, Cathy. "Dead Poets Society," *George Magazine*, October 1998.

Scruggs, Kathy and Scott Marshall. "Witness Says Off-Duty Cops Fired First Shot; Claims Rapper's Return Fire Caused Brothers' Wounds," *Atlanta Journal-Constitution*,
November 3, 1993, p. D12.

"Sean Combs Admits to Cheating on Jennifer Lopez," *Hindustan Times*, October 23, 2006.

"Sean "Puffy" Combs Acquitted of Gun Possession and Bribery Charges," *Jet*, April 2, 2001, p. 57.

"Sean (Puffy) Combs Arrested in Beating of Record Executive,' *Ontario Record*, April 19, 1999, p. B10.

Seng, Koh Eng. "Gangsta Rap: East Coast vs. West Coast," *New Straits Times* (Malaysia), May 21, 1997, p. 6.

"Shakur Pleads Not Guilty in Shooting of 2 Officers," *Orlando Sentinel*, December 3, 1993, p. A02.

Silverman, Stephen M. "P Diddy Settles $3 Million Lawsuit; The Music Mogul Reaches a Deal with the Driver Who Sped Him and J. Lo Away From the Notorious 1999 Times Square Nightclub Shooting," *People* magazine, February 4, 2004.

Simms, Greg Jr. "Bad Boy Spanked As Arista Drops Label," *Dayton Daily News*, January 18, 2002, p. 23.

Specter, Michael. "Excess Ticket Sale May Have Caused Fatal Crush at Gym," *New York Times,* December 31, 1991, p. A01.

_____. "Dinkins Aide Faults College in Stampede; Ninth Victim Dies from Injuries at Gym," *New York Times*, January 2, 1992, p. B01.

Spector, Josh. "Sony Pictures Targeted by Inmate's Son," *Hollywood Reporter*, December 3, 2003.

Suggs, Ernie and Steve Visser. "Shootout Victims Mourned; Funeral-Goers in New York are Urged to Turn Away from Violence to Being Lifesavers," *Atlanta Journal-Constitution*, November 20, 2003, p. D01.

Sullivan, John. "Rap Producer Testifies on Fatal Stampede at City College," *New York Times*, March 24, 1998, p. B03.

Sullivan, Joseph F. "Father Questioned in Teaneck Killings; Revenge is Regarded as Crime Motive," *New York Times*, December 9, 1975.

Sullivan, Ronald. "Mother, 4 Children Are Shot to Death in Home in Teaneck," *New York Times,* December 7, 1975.

"Tupac Murder Suspect Orlando Anderson Dead," *Associated Press*, June 1, 1998.

Turner, Khary Kimani. "Mysterious: The Ways to be Wicked," *Metro Times Detroit,* March 5, 2003.

Van Gelder, Lawrence. "$600,000 Heroin Seized on 3rd Avenue; "Charlie Chan" Detectives Close in and Arrest Two," *New York Times*, June 9, 1968, p. A44.

Visser, Steve. "Club Ejected Shooting Victim; Fatal Clash Came 3 Hours after Dispute with Woman," *Atlanta Journal-Constitution*, November 13, 2003, p. F01.

_____. "Shootout in Buckhead; Double Homicide Fuels Call for Crackdown on Rowdy Bar District," *Atlanta Journal-Constitution*, November 12, 2003, p. A01.

Waggoner, Walter H. "Revenge Believed Motive In Diggs Family Slayings," *New York Times*, December 19, 1975, p 83.

_____. "A Link to Diggs Murders Sought in Harlem Slaying," *New York Times,* December 17, 1975, p. 95.
Walker, Chris J. "Stevie J," *Mix* [online magazine], November 1, 2002. http://mixonline.com/recording/interviews/audio_stevie/

Warren, Beth. "Facts Scarce in 2003 Deaths; Buckhead Nightlife Remains a Concern," *Atlanta Journal-Constitution*, January 3, 2005, p. B01.

Wartofsky, Alona. "Jury Acquits Rap's Sean "Puffy" Combs," *Washington Post*, March 17, 2001, p. A01.

Williams, Laura. "Suspect in '94 Shoot of Tupac," *New York Daily News*, October 25, 1996, p. 4.

_____. "Feds Hope to Bury King Tut," *New York Daily News*, October 27, 1996, p. 13.

Williams, Precious. "Who's A Mummy's Boy," *Mail on Sunday*, February 16, 2003, p. 39.

Younge, Gary. "Triggaz with Attitude; The Latest Bloody Installment in the US Saga of Coast-to-Coast Gangsta Rap Warfare Came Last Sunday with Another Murder," *The Guardian* (London), March 14, 1997, p. T10.

COURT CITATIONS

Eric Wright et al., v. Andre Young et al, Case No. 2:93-cv-00478-WJR-GHK, U.S. District Court, Central District of California, Western Division- Los Angeles (1993)

Estate of Christopher G.L. Wallace v. City of Los Angeles, et al. United States District Court for the Central District of California, 229 F.R.D. 163 (2005)

Jacques Agnant v. Estate of Tupac Shakur, 30 F. Supp 2d 420 (Southern District of New York) (1998)

James Sabatino v. Tracy Johns, et al. Case 5:06-cv-00353-WTH-GRJ (U.S. Dist. Ct, Mid. Dist. Florida). September 27, 2006.

James Sabatino v. Combs, et al., Case No. 1:07-cv-22638-MGC (U.S. District Court, Southern District of Florida, 2007)

Kirk Burrowes v. Sean Combs, et al., United States Court of Appeals for the Second Circuit, 124 Fed. Appx. 70 (2005)

Lydia Harris and Michael Harris v. Marion Knight Jr., Case No. LA-06-11187-EC. United States Bankruptcy Court, Central Dist of California, Los Angeles Division (2007).

Malcolm Greenidge, et al. [The Outlawz], v Death Row Records, U.S. District Ct., Central District of California. Case No. 2:00-vc-04832-JSL-AIJ (2000).

People v. Jamal Barrow, Supreme Court of New York, *6 N.Y.3d 809; 845 N.E.2d 1280 (1999).*

Robert G.A. Thompson v. 76 Corp. d/b/a Club New York et al., Supreme Court of New York. 2008 NY Slip Op 6981; 54 A.D.3d 844 (2008).

Roger Mills v. Sean Combs et al., Civ. Case No. 01-109682, Wayne County Circuit Court (Michigan) (2001).

Sharonda Davis v. Anthony McCommons, et al. Case No. 1:97-cv-03339-TWT. U.S. District Court, Northern District of Georgia (Atlanta) (1997).

United States v. Terry Lee Flenory, et al. Crim. No. 05-80955. U.S. District Court, Eastern District of Michigan (Southern Division) (2007).

United States v. Marion Hugh Knight, Crim. No. 2:95-cr-00883-WJR-1. U.S. Dist. Ct, Central Dist. Of California. (1995)

United States v. Mark Anthony Bell, Crim. No. 1:07-mj-00181-ECS-1, United States District Court, Northern District of Georgia (2007)

United States v. Mark Anthony Bell, Crim. No. 1:06-cr-00484-CMH-1, United States District Court, Eastern District of Virginia (2006)

Wardell Fenderson v. Bad Boy Entertainment Inc., et al., Supreme Court of New York (2000)

MISCELLANEOUS

"Chronicles of Junior M.A.F.I.A." Ground Zero Entertainment (DVD: 2005)

Death Certificate, State of Georgia. No. 007531. "Grady Louis Hicks aka Jason Brown. (February 27, 1996)

Death Certificate, State of Georgia. No. 042856. "Jai Hassan-Jamal Robles. (October 13, 1995)

Rodriguez, Jayson, and Sway J. Calloway. "Game Manager Jimmy Rosemond Recalls Events The Night Tupac Was Shot, Says Session Was 'All Business'". MTV News, April 1, 2008, http://www.mtv.com/news/articles/1584524/20080331/2pac.jhtml#

"Jimmy Henchmen vs. James Rosemond," August 29, 2006. http://www.hhnlive.com/features/more/101.

"Bad Boy Worldwide Entertainment Group." *Hoover's Company Records.* December 12, 2006.

Rose, Charlie. "American Gangster: The Real Story," *Charlie Rose Show*, November 2, 2007.

Franklin R. "P. Diddy's Grave Yard of Bad Boy Artists," September 1, 2008. http://filthyrag.com/blog/tag/diddy/

"Diddy's Side Chick Speaks!" [Sarah Chapman] November 29, 2006. http://www.mediatakeout.com/exclusives/Diddy_Side.html

"SR Exclusive: Sarah Chapman Speaks Out: I Want to be Heard," September 12, 2007. http://sandrarosenews.blogspot.com/2007/09/sr-exclusive-sarah-chapman-speaks-out-i.html

BLACK MAFIA FAMILY (series)

Shalhoup, Mara. "Hip-Hop's Shadowy Empire; "Big Meech" Flenory and the Black Mafia Family Were Hip-Hop Royalty. But Investigators Say They Had a Darker Side," December 6, 2006. PART 1 of 3. http://atlanta.creativeloafing.com/gyrobase/Content?oid=oid%3A164707

_____. "Hip-Hop's Shadowy Empire: Loyalty within the Black Mafia Family made the alleged drug enterprise nearly impenetrable. But one

high-placed member would break BMF's code of silence." December 13, 2006. Part 2 of 3.
http://atlanta.creativeloafing.com/gyrobase/Content?oid=oid%3A167977

_____. "Hip-Hop's Shadowy Empire; In the summer of 2005, the party would get out of hand for Demetrius "Big Meech" Flenory and the Black Mafia Family. And the feds would be ready to make their move. December 20, 2006. PART 3 of 3.
http://atlanta.creativeloafing.com/gyrobase/hip_hop_s_shadowy_empire/Content?oid=171160

_____. "BMF co-leaders sentenced; Strong show of support for Black Mafia Family's Flenory brothers," September 17, 2008.
http://atlanta.creativeloafing.com/gyrobase/bmf_co_leaders_sentenced/Content?oid=561412

_____. "BMF's judgment day; Meech pleads guilty," November 14, 2007.
http://atlanta.creativeloafing.com/gyrobase/bmf_s_judgment_day/Content?oid=337283

MARK CURRY

Baraka, Rhonda. "Words and Deeds; Handicapping the Grammys," *Billboard*, February 2, 2002, p. 45.

"Black Rob Set to Ignite Hip-Hop Scene With New Album," *Business Wire*, February 15, 2000.

Carter, Nick. "Fans Who Paid to see P. Diddy and Family Left in Dark," *Milwaukee Journal Sentinel*, August 17, 2001, p. B06.

Ferman, Dave. "Puff and Stuff; Combs' New CD a Bunch of Boastful Hot Air," *Fort Worth Star-Telegram,*" June 20, 2001, p. 20.

Flaherty, David. "Born Again Notorious B.I.G. (Bad Boy/BMG), *Sunday Herald Sun* (Melbourne), January 30, 2000, p. 74.

Gareth, Thomas. "The Bad Boy Goes Back to the Street," *Music and Media* (London), September 22, 2001, p. 3.

Goss, Latrice. "Out With the Old and In with the New; The Best of 2001 and the Best Yet to Come,' *New York Beacon*, January 23, 2002, p. 32.

"Grammy Nominees by Category," *St. Louis Post-Dispatch*, February 27, 2002, p. E06.

Liverpool, Tricia. "No Way Back; P. Diddy Faces the Music after His Trials and Tribulations," *The Voice* (Atlanta), October 1, 2001, p. 45.

Makin, Robert. "I Want My MTV Awards," *Bridgewater Courier*, August 28, 2002, p. B04.

McDonnell, Evelyn. "Region Gets Its Groove Back with DJ Summit," *Miami Herald*, October 17, 2001, p. B01.

Munson, Kyle. "P. Rates D for Dud; Diddy Should Stick to Videos," *Des Moines Register*, September 3, 2002, p. E03.

"Nominees for 2d Annual BET Awards," *United Press International*, May 15, 2002.

Robinson, Regina. "Combs Has a New Name, New Album, New Outlook on Life," *Chicago Sun-Times*, July 15, 2001, p. 13.

Simms, Greg Jr. "A Dear Sean Letter," *Dayton Daily News*," February 14, 2003, p. 5.

Thrasher, Jamal. "P. Diddy's "Saga" Sags," *Pittsburgh Post-Gazette*, August 2, 2001, p. A04.

PUFF: ROLE MODEL

I. Justin Combs Gets a Lap Dance

Puff's parenting skills were heavily criticized after these photos of his 12-year-son getting a lap dance were released.

http://www.hollywoodgrind.com/sean-combs-son-justin-gets-a-lap-dance/

II. Puff's Brain on Drugs

Video on Youtube Purporting to show Puff Under the Influence.

http://www.youtube.com/watch?v=QG1SjnHAEOs

Video of Puff allegedly buying Ecstasy pills in Ibiza.

http://www.totallycrap.com/videos/videos_p_diddy_buying_xtc_in_ibiza/